NEWSTEAD

Cameos of Eighty Years

1916 – 1996

Major Jim Gordon MBE

First Published in 1997

by Major Jim Gordon MBE

Fortune Row, Newstead, Melrose

Roxburghshire

Printed by Meigle Printers Ltd., Galashiels

ISBN 0 9531315 0 5

In memory of my wife Beryl, who defied adversity yet
willingly shared our many experiences, and loved the
Old Newstead.

For that season we must be apart
For a little length of years
Till my life's last hour nears
And above the beat of my heart
I hear her voice in my ears.

INTRODUCTION

There are advantages and disadvantages in being the oldest native-born male in an ancient and historical village, such as Newstead.

The advantages, are a certain smug pseudo feeling of satisfaction, that old memories of village life, provide an arrogant domination over Newcomers, when historical and ancient customs come under discussion. The disadvantages only become apparent, when advice on Civic matters such as, rights of way, or ancient names is requested by some new village influx, given, and then cast aside and ignored.

However, this pot-pourri of Newstead Village life during the past eighty years may serve to qualify as a vindication of the former. Compiled mostly from personal memories, with just a modicum of basic research, I am indebted for much helpful advice and guidance to Willie Cleaver in California, Jim Forrest in Grangemouth, Annie Mitchell and Adam Crawford in Melrose. Annie Mitchell's many photographs gives much added effect. The photographic assistance and expertise of Bill Young deserves special mention, and I am indebted to Peter Baillie for his help with the old poems.

I would like to thank Jean Walley who willingly accepted the arduous typing workload, for proof reading the manuscript, producing the cover design and at times correcting my repetitive tendencies, she has been indispensable to me. Her knowledge and meticulous attention to detail have been a major contribution to this final outcome. So I am deeply indebted to her.

Finally, it is to Liz Taylor, Newstead's famed authoress whose inspiration and encouragement was compelling enough to overcome my natural reluctance, that a very special credit must go.

Jim Gordon

THE OLD MEN

This is our lot if we live so long and labour unto the end
That we outlive the impatient years and the much too patient friend
And because we know we have breath in our mouth and think we have thoughts in
*   our head.*

We shall assume that we are alive, whereas we are really dead.
This is our lot if we live so long and listen to those who love us
That we are shunned by the people about, and shamed by the powers above us
Wherefore be free of your harness betimes, but being free be assured,
That he who hath not endured to the death from his birth hath never endured.

Rudyard Kipling

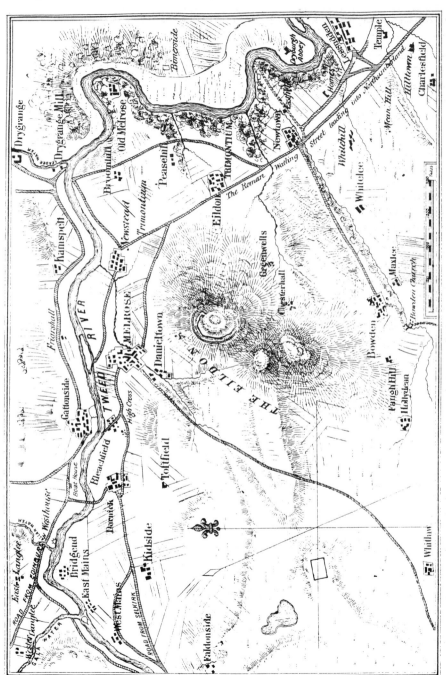

This plan shows Newstead and the surrounding area in 1793. It is interesting that Trimontium is shown in two separate locations.

CONTENTS

AULD NEWSTEID

SHOULD AULD ACQUAINTANCE BE FORGOT?

Newstead is often proclaimed as the oldest inhabited village in Scotland. What does all this really mean?

For a start, we are well aware that the Roman Centurions of Agricola's army of occupation descended upon Newstead and established the Fort of Trimontium in the first century AD.

At that time the tribe referred to by the Romans as Selgovians, occupied a fortified settlement on the eastern Eildon Hill. On the Mediterranean island of Capri, the Roman Emperor Tiberius, at the Villa Jovi was enjoying the delights of concubines and debauchery, worshipping the God of Bacchus, only to be interrupted by the alarming news from Rome, of the crucifixion and resurrection of Jesus Christ.

The Newstead Roman occupation undoubtedly attracted a camp follower element, and the feeling today is that this was instrumental in the establishment of Newstead as a community. The withdrawal of the Romans from North Britain, after fully one hundred years of frontier warfare, perhaps left behind a settlement too well established to contemplate dispersal.

The gap of historical continuity then widens, and there seems to have been little attempt, or inclination to record subsequent events, until the arrival of St. Aiden and his monks, followed by St. Cuthbert, in the year 657. The first Abbot of Melrose was Eata and under him St. Boisil, or Boswell, from which the village of St. Boswells takes its name.

With the monks to help build the Abbey, came architects and artisans with skills in building, unknown to the native workers of that time. Their ability to teach such crafts, and the willingness of the local populace who we know, when we observe their handiwork on Melrose Abbey, became extremely proficient, perhaps led to the establishment in Newstead of the famous colony of Masons. Certainly the first Masonic Lodge was established by them, in St. John's Wynd,

Newstead. The exact date is in doubt, but in 1675, when a "mutual agreement" was drawn up, to increase from four to seven years the period of apprenticeship to the trade, eighty signatures of Masons and employers were recorded, suggesting a substantial proportion of villagers at that time were active in the profession.

When this predominantly Masonic era declined, a weaving community became established, with their bleach field at the Yiddy, so Newstead's population diversified for a time, but the demise of the weaving industry remains obscure and unrecorded.

A much more recent influx of Irish labourers during the construction of the railway system, although only for a few years, has not, as one would expect had any significant impact.

The purpose therefore of this short treatise is to arrest the trend in abandoned history, by recording some aspects of the village lifestyle since 1916, which are gone but not forgotten.

SALAD DAYS IN NEWSTEAD

A fickle memory is a common enough expression, so when an old man replies, "I doot a 'dinna ken", he may be indicating a loss of memory, or perhaps a lack of knowledge. Either way the definite line is obscure. But I find in my case, a recall of incidents are more likely to be of very early youth, whilst more recent experiences escape my memory entirely.

Thus my first recollections began at about the age of two. I was born in 1916, at Fortune Row, where I still live today, eighty years on. As my father, like others, was serving in the Great War, my mother, whether out of boredom, or for financial reasons took a job as housekeeper at Mellerstain. Together then, we took a train from Melrose Station to Newtown, which was the junction for Earlston station. I remember crossing the Leaderfoot Viaduct and arriving at Earlston station where we were met by what may have been a taxi. The vehicle was open, without a hood, and the driver, a girl with long blonde hair. It was so long that sitting in the rear seat with mother, the hair was blowing into my face as we travelled the few miles to Mellerstain.

My memories of Mellerstain, are of being put to bed in a warm room, watching the flickering flame of a fire reflected on the walls. The long walk from the House, and the stone stairway to the edge of the lake, and the swans feeding at the lakeside. I'm sure there was also a blue painted rowing boat. I seemed to have had a lisp at that time, as having been caught sampling green peas I was forced to say sorry to Hume, which I pronounced "Thume". I have no other recollections. We returned to Newstead, and my father came home on leave. On his departure to the War Front, Mother and I were on Melrose station platform. The train seemed full of men leaning out of the windows, but my main interest at that time, was in a crate of goats on the station forecourt. I was interrupted by Mother, saying "wave, wave" and by the time I had turned around, the train was disappearing round the bend, and my father waving back. I also remember lots of picnics on the Eildon Hills, when water was boiled

3

in a tin kettle, and the problem we had avoiding vicious red ants, and picking Buttercups in the long meadow between the back road and the railway line.

An old photograph shows me in pantaloons at about two or three years old. Other memories are of a large white pig in a pig sty at the top of Claymires lane, and masses of piglets fighting for a place by her side, the fan trained plum trees on the front walls of Fortune Row, and the large Victorian plum tree by the burn. By now I must have been about three and Mother, unknown of course to me, was expecting the birth of my brother, and she rested in the afternoons. I still remember the quiet stillness in the house, and the only sound to be heard was the tick, tock of the clock. In 1920 my brother was born. Babies at that time were delivered at home, and my Mother had the services of a nurse, probably a District Nurse called Nurse Wilkinson who had actually lived with us, before and after the birth. She had a peculiar, probably Newcastle accent, and became a great friend, keeping up a contact with Mother for many years afterwards. I expect Dr McMillan who lived at St John's in Melrose attended. He removed my tonsils on the kitchen table at home. I remember so well the horrid taste of chloroform, and a Mr Gibson from Galashiels arriving with black grapes from the famous vineyard at Clovenfords. My brother was christened at home in Fortune Row, by the Reverend Robert James (Robbie) Thompson, a very popular and well liked Minister, who was very friendly with my parents. Mother was an accomplished cook, and I remember a gathering of neighbours, and the table full of cakes and scones.

Robbie Thompson also had christened me, and I was presented with a Bible suitably inscribed by him. I don't think my brother was so treated. Many years later, forty eight, to be exact Mr Thompson although then retired, and having a special dispensation from the Church of Scotland, christened my daughter, Barbara, in the Manse, in a silver Roman bowl which he and Dr James Curle had unearthed at Trimontium during the excavations there in 1910. The bowl was on loan from the Queen Street museum in Edinburgh. Barbara has my Bible in Italy now.

In The Beginning

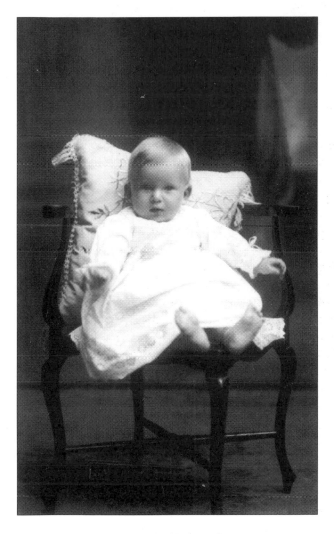

Life at Fortune Row
1916

"FAIRFAX"

NEWSTEAD'S HISTORICAL CONNECTION

Old Newstead, long a kaleidoscope of historical memories, embracing Romans, ancient Masonic cultures, and even the descent of Meteorites, has now erased one of its final connections with contemporary history, i.e. "Fairfax".

It was generally thought, by we few survivors of the Fairfax era, who were of course but children at that time, that the Library, Deaconess' House, Mission Hall and Reading Room had been donated to the village by Admiral Fairfax. However, this is not so. The bequest was the desire of his widow, Dame Harriet Kinloch or Fairfax, in memory of her late husband Sir Henry Fairfax, and specifically for the spiritual and social well being of the community of Newstead. This was put in train in 1901.

Admiral Fairfax, up to the time of his death in 1900 resided at Ravenswood. It is not clear when he first came, but Ravenswood itself was occupied until the time of his death in 1831 by Major John Scott. This gentleman was a brother to the Laird of Raeburn, who had made a fortune in the East Indies, and bestowed the name of Ravenswood on the villa he had built there. He suffered badly from asthma.

Admiral Fairfax was born in Edinburgh, on 21st January 1837 and entered the Royal Navy in 1850. He had an illustrious career, commanding at various times HM ships, VOLAGE, BRITANNIA and MONARCH. He also served in AMPHITRITE on two voyages to the Arctic and Bering Strait. Whilst serving in the AERIAL on the South East Coast of Africa, he distinguished himself especially in the capture of a piratical slave trading ship. For this action of great gallantry, he was promoted from Lieutenant to Commander. During the Egyptian war in 1882, he took part in the bombardment of Alexandria. As well as ADC to the Queen, he was also Commander in Chief of the Australian Station, and later commander of the Channel Squadron, Royal Navy.

Unfortunately, one of his ships, the HOWE became stranded in the entrance to Ferrol harbour and he was tried by Court Martial in December 1882, but acquitted. This appears to have been the sole blemish in his remarkable career. Promoted Admiral on 10th May 1899, he became Commander in Chief at Devonport Royal Navy Base, Devonport. After ten months in this command and for health reasons he departed for Naples. He died of a stroke while driving in a carriage to the Hotel Continental in Naples on March 20th 1900. The body was embalmed and brought back for internment in the family vault at Maxton. The large white marble bust of Sir Henry which originally stood in the Fairfax Hall grounds and which is now located in Newstead Village Hall was commissioned and executed by an Italian sculptor in Naples. The signature being recorded at the base. He was aged 62. The funeral took place on 25th April 1900, on a very wintry day of snow showers and a biting wind. The cortège left Ravenswood at noon, escorted by the Melrose Company of the Border Rifles, in full dress uniform, under command of Major Small, and a detachment of Royal Navy Bluejackets from HMS CALEDONIA at Queensferry, under command of Lieutenant Meiklejohn. The journey from Ravenswood to Maxton by march route took one and a half hours.

Arriving at Maxton House gate at one thirty p.m. Among the many mourners were the Ravenswood household staff and retainers, including the gardeners, Yea and Short. During his sojourn in the Pacific the Admiral collected exotic seeds and plants and Mr Yea's task was to propagate those at Ravenswood. Sir Henry was at that time also a Fellow of the Royal Geographic Society. Following his death the naval officers at Davenport decided to erect, in his honour, a memorial which took the form of a furnished room at the Royal Sailors home at Davenport, and a brass memorial tablet.

In 1901 his widow, Dame Harriet Kinloch or Fairfax, then residing in London, made a decision in honour of her late husband's memory to provide, for the Newstead residents, a library, reading room and Mission Hall. This ambitious project surprisingly was to be for the "Communities of Newstead, Leaderfoot, Eildon, Newtown and other adjacent parts, being all parts of the Parish of Melrose". Lady Fairfax's first task was to appoint trustees and some interesting and well known individuals were chosen. They were, the Reverend Robert James Thompson, Minister of Melrose Parish Church, James

Henderson of Broomielees, James Curle of Harleyburn, James Tocher of Beechgrove, George Hunter of Blyth, Thomas Fairbairn of Weirhill Place, Melrose, William Curle, Baker, High Street, Melrose, John Renwick, Nursery and Seedsman Melrose, John Brown, Miller of Newstead, James Linton, gardener Drygrange, Robert Lindsay, Market Gardener Darnick, Andrew Mclaren, Baker Melrose and Charles Redpath, Gattonside, the latter being a member of the Kirk Session Melrose Parish.

The grand design was that certain subjects in Newstead acquired by her from Sir Henry's Trustees and which he had owned in Newstead, augmented by the purchase of adjacent properties should allow for provision of a Mission Hall, Reading Room and Library. It appears that this centred on the small piece of ground in the centre of Newstead known by the name of Cromarty, presumably the area later known as the Fairfax Hall.

Some of the adjacent properties bore quaint titles, Middlingstead and Vicarage Teind, obviously long forgotten. The stipulations laid down by her Ladyship were also for the erection of a Deaconess's House and a pledge to provide boundary fences, water and drainage pipes, paper and painting, blinds, grates and bells, and the laying out of the grounds. This house in my time known as Deaconess House was built about 1902 or 1903. It is quite distinctive in its colonial style, with red tiled roof, being the only one of its type in the village.

In my youth the Deaconesses were Miss McCartney and Miss Sewel, but I think also there was a third. Lady Fairfax also agreed to pay the sum of forty pounds per annum, paid half yearly in advance towards the salary of the Deaconess. Also, she agreed to transfer twenty-six, seven percent, cumulative Preference Shares of five pounds each of the Brompton and Kensington Electricity Supply Company, the half yearly dividend from which to meet the rates, taxes and cleaning of the Mission hall. The Trustees were given the power to allow the hall keeper free occupation of the premises as part of his or her remuneration.

Thus Mrs Cleaver occupied the two storey house, now demolished, which stood at the entrance to the Fairfax Hall. The Deaconess, Parish Sister Missionary or Licentiate of the Church of Scotland to be appointed was, as part of the employment, to carry on the Newstead Mothers' meeting, and to look after the Girls Friendly

Society. Additionally, to take charge of Newstead Library and Reading Room. The Trustees additional responsibilities was the purchase for the Library and Reading Room, books, periodicals, pamphlets, papers, games etc., and to charge members for the use of the Reading Room, and Library as they thought fit.

Fairfax Hall

The services in the Mission Hall were to be of Protestant origin, Church of Scotland, Episcopal, and the United Free Church, and they had powers, if thought fit to let the Mission Hall and Deaconess House for summer quarters. To allow for the erection of the Deaconess House "Mud Miles" pub and adjoining dwelling houses were demolished and a retaining wall built. This house now known as Fairfax was unique in that the interior walls were adorned in large gold lettering with writing from the scriptures and the Commandments. The extensive garden contained many fruit trees and in 1920 in my youth, the Deaconesses harvested the results. One particularly tall pear tree at the South West corner of the house, produced massive crops each year, and the pears freely distributed to us children by the Deaconess.

The Mission Hall was an attractive building of wood and brick on a cement base. It had an imposing entrance porch, a well kept gravel approach, surrounded by lawns and landscaped with unusual trees. On the East side were Yew trees and the marble bust of Sir Henry protected and shielded by a covered wooden erection. On the South and West were Acacias, Laburnum, and many unknown species plus Yellow Holly and a very tall Weeping Elm. The Hall had a corrugated roof and a brass commemorative plate. The interior furnishings, included wooden ash chair and forms, linen curtains, a platform or stage, organ, goose necked reading lamps with green shades and attractive brass hanging paraffin lamps. There were also many bound volumes of the Illustrated London News. The Hall was much in demand at that time.

The Deaconesses taught at Sunday school which we all attended regularly. I remember whilst awaiting the Deaconess to descend the stairs from the house, cleaning my pennies in the earth under the trees in order to make them appear more presentable. I remember also, the concerts by Mr Willie Rankine's concert party from Galashiels, and Meg Hart and her sister, well known vocalists from Melrose. There were many others. Mrs Cleaver and her family Beatrice, John and Willie lived as caretaker in the House which stood at the road entrance gates. The Hall grounds were beautifully kept. The chairs and forms scrubbed white, the gravel well raked and free from weeds and the grass cut regularly, all a great credit to them.

After the first World War, a memorial to the dead was erected in the Hall grounds immediately opposite the school entrance, now of course the Village Hall. A portion of the retaining wall was cut away and protective wrought iron railings erected to assist visibility. Dubiety, exists however regarding the Library and Reading Room. In my young days Library Cottage in St John's Wynd was occupied by Mr William Clark and his wife, who were Mrs Cleaver's parents. He had come from Leaderfoot and was by trade a joiner. I do not recall a Library there and the house size does not suggest accommodation for both a dwelling house, Library and Reading Room. If it was the Library, it was certainly not built at the time of the Fairfax Mission Hall and Deaconess' House as it adjoins Tweed View. Both appeared in old village photographs of the pub and dwelling houses. Also, the presence in the Mission Hall books and magazines suggests the Hall at some time incorporated the Reading Room. Only perusal of Library Cottage title deeds can clarify the position.

Due to the changing styles of entertainment and the evolving patterns of village life, the Fairfax Hall became, like so much else, a casualty of the times, with its usefulness, community association, and attractions sadly diminished. The Church of Scotland carried the burden and eventually a decision was made to dispose of the properties, so nobly bequeathed to the village by Dame Harriet Fairfax. The Deaconess House and Fairfax Cottage were sold along with the Mission Hall. The Hall briefly converted for a knitting machine venture, was finally demolished and the furniture sold to a community centre in Musselburgh. The Caretaker's house was then demolished and the Old War Memorial moved and re-sited to an inaccessible position by the road side. The grounds so gratefully presented to the village have passed subsequently to a property developer with the drastic results so obvious today.

Thus Newstead has severed connections with Fairfax, and all this, within a contemporary lifetime. This, an object lesson, on the pitfalls attendant on benevolent and well meaning bequests, which appear to be secure, but are so often the subject of calculating and scheming, thus negating the original purpose.

THE FLOUR MILL

Newstead Mill was built sometime during the early part of the nineteenth century. It had the outward appearance of two stories, but descending many indoor stairs to the water wheel and water level, gave an inside impression of at least three or four.

The mill was run on water from the Tweed, deflected by a sluice gate turnscrew at Melrose Cauld, which proceeded first to work the Abbey Mill at Melrose, then on to Newstead via what was known as The Dam, being the mill stream. At Newstead there was a mechanism and hake, whereby the water flowed under the Annay Road, to activate the mill wheel or, when not required, to allow the water to by-pass the wheel and proceed onwards down the dam and re-enter the Tweed by the Yiddy.

The large wheel was of cast iron, with wooden panels. When in motion this operated a system of long broad leather belts, passing from the bottom through apertures in the various floors, to the very top, all working at once. The belts and machinery were unprotected and apparently not considered a danger, even to us as children.

There was also a very large domed tin kiln, heated by a coke fire where oats were dried in the making of oat meal. This also had a ventilator to allow moisture to escape. The Brown family had just given up the mill and Bell was the Miller in my time. Bell had a large family of boys, who all worked at the milling, and I don't remember any outside assistance employed.

The Bells' must have been extremely tolerant of us children, as we had free access every where. It is surprising that there were no accidents with so much unprotected machinery, constantly on the move. It really was a fascinating place. Being built on sloping ground, there were a series of outside cement steps with iron handrails, and an extending hoist and pulley on the top floor for accepting grain etc. for milling. Why it should all go to the top at first, remains a mystery. I only remember corn and Indian corn or maize, but never wheat. Each floor seemed to be milling different products, some white fine flour, some brown, others, coarse meal

12

and of course oat meal. Everything was covered in white dust or powder.

The kiln was for drying and roasting the oats for oat meal, and was the most popular and frequented part for us, as we were allowed to collect handfuls of the warm meal, edible and very appetising.

Whatever was milled, was finally collected by the arrival of flat horse drawn carts, which were backed into the loading bay at the Annay Road end.

The photograph, date unknown, shows the Old Newstead Mill House, with part of the Mill showing on the left. Violet Brown is the child held on her mother's knee.

The Mill House, where the Bells' lived, was at the east end and the front door opened on to the Main Road. They had one daughter, Bessie, who was courted by Tom Mitchell from St John's. He played rugby on Saturdays, and on one particular day, when I was about nine or ten years old, I was walking down the village, behind him on his way to Melrose. When he reached the area opposite Bell's front door, Bessie dashed out, had a few words, then proceeded to kiss him, all in the middle of the roadway. Being naive, and never having witnessed kissing before, this was a culture shock, which remains with me today.

The mill however, provided a necessary service, and the Millers remuneration in retaining a percentage of the production ensured against a problem of bad debts. All of us survivors, who remember the mill, retain the most fond affections.

There is really nothing like it around today!

SONG OF NEWSTEAD

by

Piper Jamie Gordon

To the tune "Dear Tae Me"

While lookin doon ower Newstead Mill,
a hamely sicht to me.
The sun sets red ower Meigle hill,
It warms ma hairt tae see,
For roond this countryside I kent,
Ilk dyke an' hedge an' tree.
T'was here ma happy youth was spent,
T'will aye be dear to me.

❖ ❖ ❖

Noo lovely flo'ers begin tae spring,
The daffodills are comin'
The bees are a' noo on the wing,
I hear their constant hummin',
An' there the little lambs at play,
in that wee field I see,
Ana' a' these sichts an' soons I'll say
will aye be dear tae to me.

❖ ❖ ❖

Noo natures airy concert rings, Wi' sprichtly glee before us,
The blackie finest bird that sings,
Will join in ready chorus.
An' hark at that the mavis tae'
Upon oor aulf ploom tree,
Sic pleasures here I'm bound to say,
Will Aye be dear te me.

15

Tae walk doon by the Yiddy ther,
An' by the damside green,
By Millmount up the Tweedside fair,
Up tae the Battery stream.
Or climmin up the Eildon Hill,
Wad gleddin ony e'e,
Tae look ower Newstead is a thrill,
Thats' aye sae dear tae me.

The hooses noo are getting spent,
An' some hae crummelt sair,
Indeed a lot o' them hae went,
Far far beyond repair.
But when I end my days indeed,
Thats' where I want tae be,
In that wee village by the Tweed
Thats' aye sae dear tae me.

THE YIDDY

HERITAGE ABANDONED

This is an area of Newstead Common Land lying between the Village on the north side, and the river Tweed, gifted to the village by Admiral Fairfax of Ravenswood. The road from the village known to the villagers as the Yiddy road, was however referred to in 1921 Church Magazine notes, by the Reverend Robbie Thompson as the Yeddy.

While its origins are lost in history, it was known to have been a bleach field in days long past. It is also a fact that a fabric called Melrose Land Linen was produced in the area, and later cotton weaving, so there is the possibility of a connection.

The origin of this name for the area of Common Land, north of the village up to the Tweed boundary, is obscure, and lost in time.

My personal speculation relates to the fact that the first house on the Yiddy Road, is Addey Cottage. Addey, in my young days was an affectionate term for Adam. The Adam and Yid connection produces Yid or Yiddy. Nobody can be sure, but in any case, local busy bodies have changed the road from the village to the Tweed, to Eddy Road.

The current village population largely comprised of newcomers, appears unaware that this village possession has a name at all. So much then for a conservation village. Being a bleach field, presumably this was where the old colony of Newstead Weavers put the finishing touches to their handiwork.

In the 1920's, the Yiddy was a popular gathering spot for the villagers, young and old. Almost every activity took place there. Miss Cowan, the village schoolmistress, taught us nature study. People held picnics. Boys played games and the Crighton Cup Rugby team trained and prepared there as well. At Easter, when old customs compelled mothers to produce boiled eggs coloured by Dolly Dye Blue, or dark tea, the younger element rolled their eggs at the Yiddy. In winter, sledding was possible for the younger children, and skating on the pond for the others. The pond was a winter feature only, as it developed from flooding of the Tweed. During the summer, digging for Iron Nuts was popular, as the nuts were edible. There was also a wooden seat to rest on.

Jock Davidson, who had a small farm at Rothesay Cottage, mowed the Yiddy and the area across the Dam, up to the Boiler by the style, and made hay for his milk cows. It was always smart and tidy, even when dotted with small hay ricks. Difficult to visualise this when one looks at the mess in the Yiddy today.

Bottles left by uncaring fishermen, and the left overs from partially burned bonfires, with overgrowth and deep rutted car tracks, it presents a forlorn and neglected appearance, which should shame our village conservation committee. Unfortunately, nobody cares about the poor old Yiddy nowadays.

The Yiddy was the principal access to the Tweed, for fishers and walkers, and the riverside walk up to the west end of the Battery Dyke was a popular playground for children, wading in the river, catching minnows in the minnow pools, or bathing. The main bathing pool for the bigger boys was of course the deep water of the Boiler, and this was the Mecca for almost the entire summer months, which seemed, in those days, to be endlessly sunny. Newstead villagers had the privilege of free fishing from the Boiler down river to the mouth of the Dam. There also was a low wall of concrete to prevent river bank erosion running roughly from the present day shelter to the Dam confluence with the Tweed. It is now invisible, being covered by silt and overgrowth.

The Nirvana of the Yiddy however, had a less pleasant detraction. At that time there was no organised village refuse collection, so disposal of ashes and rubbish fell to the individual. Many houses had middens, emptied periodically when horse drawn carts appeared, and the clearances transported to a dumping ground at the Dam and Tweed junction. Three middens I remember, were at Cairnhill, Drewen Cottage and Burnfoot Cottage, today's names of course. However, Riddell, the farmer at Town Head had a special dump in a gully between fields at the top of the Hazeldean right of way. Some times it was spread on to the surrounding fields, where odd pieces of coloured broken crockery are still to be found today, sometimes confused as Roman Pottery.

The Yiddy refuse dump grew quickly, as people carried every thing in barrows and other conveyances. Rats were attracted and colonised the area in large numbers. Village boys scavenged and searched through the discarded material, unhygienic as it was, for thrift prevailed in those hard times. Strangely, similar behaviour in the 1990's, by many well to do adults transformed Riddell's old field dump into a present day paradise for scavengers. Some things never change!

However, the Yiddy refuse tip was cunningly sited, because when the truly immense floods of those times occurred, the entire structure simply disappeared down stream.

The rats survived and could be seen high in the hawthorn hedges, until the water receded.

One particular summer flood, of gigantic proportions, I remember to this day. After day's of heavy rain, the Tweed rose rapidly, and divided into two, opposite the Boiler on the Kittyfield side, breaking through and along the front of the Fir Wood and Heronry. Tom Porteus from Leaderfoot farm, had a mixture of sheep and cattle grazing there, and they became completely cut off. Tom Porteus attempted a rescue which became hopeless. The water was rising rapidly, and the dry area grew gradually less and less.

The river was a raging brown torrent, racing at great speed, bringing down trees, battens, wooden boxes, hen houses with live hens on the top, field gates, scaffolding, trestles, etc. We villagers gathered on the high ground, could only watch with much concern, first the poor sheep forced to take to the water in panic, followed shortly by the cattle. To this day, my abiding memory, is of brown heads of the cattle, swimming for life, being swept away with absolutely no hope of survival. I believe there were also large stock losses elsewhere during that particular flood.

The Yiddy was also the starting point for some of the adolescents netting the Dam for fish. The Dam, because of the mill workings, and strong water flow, was not overgrown as it is today. The water was fresh and clear and attracted fish of all sorts. Some even found their way to the pond at the foot of the Eildons, by the golf course, by traversing via the Dam and the Malt House burn, all the length of the way up Dingleton. The net was stretched across the water, being held by young men on each bank, and one wading behind, and moving up the water flow to be stopped at the Dam, where the fish were trapped, if the sluice gates were closed.

Many fine fish were netted. This was illegal, and not acceptable to the Water Bailiff's who patrolled the rivers actively then, so suitable precautions and timing were essential for success.

In those happy days, certainly the Yiddy was the place to be.

This group on the Yiddy Road at the entrance to Rothsay Cottage show Granny Davidson and Mrs Ballantyne at the rear. Front from left: Jenny Gill, Sonny Mitchell, Annie Mitchell, May Riddell and Ella Gill.

PEOPLE I KNEW

Early in 1920, Peter Nisbet took up residence with his wife, daughter Meg and a large St Bernard dog, at the 'Auld Hoose' in Newstead. Peter, in his early days had been a joiner in Melrose and a contemporary of Billy Dodds who owned a joiners business at Fordel, off Abbey Street.

However, at some time he left Melrose to improve his lot, finally settling in Canada, at Manitoba, in the state of Saskatchewan. On retiring and having accumulated some savings, he returned to end his days in Newstead, although not known as a native. He made, as was to be expected of a former tradesman, various alterations to the external wood work, often subjected to ribald criticism from Billy Dodds when passing by.

The remnants of an old red sandstone sundial in the wall of the Auld Hoose opposite the War Memorial, was built in, when the outside stairway to the road was removed. This occurred when Peter converted the top and bottom dwellings into one. The sundial facing north was not intended then to be an effective measurement of time.

Whatever the outside work merited, the interior was less fortunate, as the handrail on the stairs to the attic was an improvised ancient wooden curtain rail, and the attic flooring consisted of discarded herring boxes. Daughter Meg was an adult spinster of wild behaviour, gauche and extrovert, and smoked heavily.

An older semi-eccentric individual, fond of a drink, employed at the Dingleton Asylum, attempted courtship often, but without notable success. Like many of the asylum staff, then, Piper McKenzie as he was known, was a highlander from the far north, and spoke in the stilted peculiar accent of the Islanders. The courting was subject to village discussion, and McKenzie stood much teasing, as he was never allowed to enter the house, so that what ever went on, took place in the walled garden, and obvious to prying interested eyes.

As the years passed, the enthusiasm faded.

The old Nisbets died and Meg still alone, lived in reclusive, straightened circumstances, always begging for cigarettes, until she was unable to cope on her own. Although there was a bath in the house the story goes that the water supply was not connected. So, when Meg, after fifteen years or so alone, was taken to hospital, the first priority obviously was a bath. Unfortunately the shock resulted in sudden death.

Certainly Meg Nisbet will remain in our memory as a Newstead character. An unusual situation for a woman of that time.

When I was very young, old Tom Mitchell lived at No. 3 St John's Cottage. He was a short stout individual. The Mitchell's had a large family of five boys and two girls. The eldest son, John James, was killed during the First Great War, serving as a Sergeant in the Black Watch, so to me, Tom Mitchell appeared as an old man. He used to tell us tales of his army days in India, living in tents and the problems they had with thieves. The standard practice, when inside the tent was to await a searching hand appearing under the tent flap, then pierce it with a bayonet.

He may have been at some time a regular soldier, but certainly he never appeared to work. He was a keen capable fisherman, carried a shotgun, and was a bosom poaching pal of Jock Pringle. They were inseparable, and the contrast in physical appearances, Tom short and fat, with Jock tall and slim often attracted amused comment.

Poaching in those days was endemic, and included rabbits, pheasants, ducks, partridges, pigeons and of course salmon. They had a poaching monopoly, undisguised, and anyone prompted to intrude on their territory was made decidedly unwelcome. Even otters came into this category.

One thought to be dead was brought back by Jock in a state of bravado, and dropped on the living room floor. During the jollification with admiring neighbours, the otter recovered sharply, only to be finally despatched by heavy blows to the floor and blood spattered over the wall paper.

One memory remains of Tom Mitchell fishing on the Millmount Haugh, when casting his line, and with a herd of bullocks near by, he accidentally hooked one in the tail. The animal obviously felt the hook, and took off, so Tom, anxious not to lose his rod and cast, followed at a run, towed along shouting, "whoa, you bugger, whoa!"

Later in life, he moved from St John's Cottage, and spent his last days at Plain Tree Cottage at the top of St John's Wynd.

THE VILLAGE SCHOOL

In my day, education commenced at the age of four, in the Village School at Newstead. The youngest members sat at the rear of the class. In 1920 there were twenty seven children attending, of different ages. The school, now the Village Hall, in the Main Street was at that time on three levels. The small playground and overhead shelter was also the entrance, one step up to a larger cloakroom containing a stove for central heating, then a further two steps up to the main classroom. There was an open fire, where the teacher stood. The caretaker was Mrs Forrest who lived at Eildon View. The entrance gate was of open iron work and could be locked, and was further enclosed by a low wall, with spiked iron railings. There were also two separate   lavatories, one at the east end for the girls, and another for the boys at the west end. Pupils ranged from four years to seven, at which age we were sent off to the larger school at Melrose. In 1920, when I started there were twenty seven pupils at Newstead school.

The catchment area included those children of the domestic staffs and household retainers of the big houses of Drygrange, Gledswood, Ravenswood and the communities of Old Melrose, Leaderfoot and Broomhill where many farm workers lived. They all walked to school. At that time in Newstead, there were many large families, the largest being fifteen Andersons at Rose Cottage in the Back Road. The Mitchells of St John's Cottage had a family of eight, and the Riddells of Town Head Farm had seven. Many others were of four and three.

The teacher in my time was a Miss Cowan. Later a Miss Erskine replaced her and she lodged with Mrs McGinnis, who lived in Claymires Cottage, now owned by Andrew Young. Classwork was done on slates, with slate pencils. When new they were an attractive grey colour, wrapped half way up in paper. I can still remember the squeaking of the pencils on the slate, all to be rubbed out with a wet rag, or handkerchief. After learning to write on slates we were promoted to copy books with pen and ink. The ink wells were sunk in the desks, I think there were also some shiny old maps on the school walls lowered by a pole when required. We were summoned by a bell. The original being still in the Village Hall today. There was also an ancient octagonal clock which sadly has not survived. Its loss though was due to improper control, long after the school was closed. It was allowed to be removed by the husband of the then lady secretary of the Village committee who claimed that it could be repaired. The clock has not been seen since.

At some time the school, due to a scarlet fever epidemic, was closed for three weeks. Local pupils who had the fever were taken as patients, to the Newstead Fever Hospital, where we who were more fortunate used to assemble on the road way to Leaderfoot and from where they could be seen in beds by the window. The TB patients slept outside on the verandahs then too. Newstead hospital was fully staffed, with a Matron and nurses, who lived on the premises in the Nurses Home at the entrance. Now occupied as Health Board offices. Miss Cowan, the school teacher cycled daily from her home in Gattonside. She came via the Kittyfield Road to Leaderfoot and up the Boat Brae to Newstead. This always surprised me, as the chain suspension bridge at Melrose was then in use. She was a remarkable person, although I do not recall much of her teaching.

Looking back at what I always thought was unusual at that age, was being introduced to the poetic works of John Keats. Mary Riddell a few years older, was also instrumental, and I remember so clearly today, the first line of Keats' "Old Meg she was a gypsy and lived upon the moor. Her bed it was the brown heath turf and her house was out of doors". Miss Cowan's nature study walks down the Yiddy to Tweedside remain forever in my memory, when she taught us the names of the many wild meadow flowers. Red Campion, Crosswort, Marsh Marigold, Cranesbill, Meadow Sweet and many others, which have never been forgotten. For some reason she called me "Pixie". On Empire Day I was chosen to represent Canada, decorated with red Maple leaves. School photographs were taken each year, in the grounds of the Fairfax Hall.

I have three particular memories viewed from the school gates of the horse drawn charabancs in convoy full of Americans coming down through the village, having visited Sir Walter Scott's grave at Dryburgh. These were the cause of some excitement. The cabs were drawn by four horses, with a cabby in top hat and long whip, and on top about twelve Americans with others inside the cab.

Another wonderment was the Holiday Fellowship passing through. This group occupied St Mary's school at the term time holidays, and were numbered in hundreds. It seems they enjoyed long rambles or journeys and they came through Newstead in straggling groups, of men and women in some bizarre dress styles. Shorts, highly coloured shirts worn by both males and females were unusual at that time. They occupied St. Mary's school for a month, but the parties changed every two weeks or so, and were obviously all English people.

Also at that time huge whole trees came through the village, on the way to the saw mill at Earlston, owned by Brownlee. The trees were on a long flat cart pulled by six strong Clydesdale horses and all chained together. The steep gradient was a terrible problem in Newstead, and often when reaching the brow of the hill at Tweedview it became too much for the poor horses. The sight of huge horses falling down, entangled in chains with bleeding knees and terror in their eyes haunts me even today. Animals in distress always upset me as a boy. The men in charge kept wooden blocks handy to put under the wheels to prevent everything from running backwards, but re-starting forward momentum with tired and injured horses became very difficult. Of course any route to Earlston involved steep gradients so there really was no easy way there. Such are my early memories of life at Newstead school.

NEWSTEAD SCHOOL

1920

Back Row: Left to Right
? Andrew Scott, Tom White, John Forrest, John Riddell,
Fred Mitchell, Arthur Anderson, Willie Anderson, Archie Anderson, ?.

Centre Row:
May Mitchell, Margaret Douglas, Grace Douglas, ? Chris Gray,
Beatrice Cleaver, ?, ?, May Riddell, ?

Front Row:
Jim Gordon, Adam Mitchell, Jean Tait, ? Tait, Annie Scott,
Molly Lowrie, ?, Bert Clark, Jim Forrest.

NEWSTEAD VILLAGE SCHOOL

1922

Back Row: Left to Right
Bert Clark, Mamie Douglas, Adam Mitchell, Andrew Scott,
Duncan McKinnon, Nellie Anderson, Willie Anderson.

Centre Row: Left to Right
Archie Anderson, Tom White, Jim Gordon, Annie Scott,
Molly Lowrie, May Riddell, Margaret Tait..

Front Row: Left to Right
Nettie Tait, Netta Purdom, Eddie Douglas, John Cleaver, Jim Forrest, May
Mitchell, ?, ?, Margaret Douglas.

BLOODY JANUARY AGAIN

In the early 1920's, the various seasons of the year appeared more stable and predictable than they are today, with very long hot summers, and very severe cold winters.

An indication of this is the numerous curling ponds then in existence. Melrose, St Boswells, Lauder and Stow, and many other towns had curling clubs all active during the winter. There were also many skating rinks.

The Melrose curling pond was at the foot of the West Eildon Hill on the common grazing land, now occupied by the Melrose Golf Club. The Melrose skating pond, situated at the east end of the Gibson Park stood roughly where the Medical Centre offices at St Dunstan's are today.

The large compensation pond on Bowden Moor, which supplied water to the Dingleton Asylum, when frozen over was popular. I do remember one Bonspiel when all the Border Curling Clubs assembled for a competition there, and hundreds of spectators and teams were on the ice. Trestle tables dispensing whisky being a prominent feature.

As the Caledonian Curling Club, the superior governing body, require, for safety reasons, that Bonspiel ice must be eight inches in thickness, some indication of the frost then prevailing can be gauged.

In Newstead skating at the Yiddy Pond was possible at times of flooding, but Newstead boys most often turned up at the Gibson Park, where water was permanent and well patronised by the sporting element within the Melrose community, when it was frozen over.

However, the most popular winter past time in Newstead was sledding. The steep hill throughout the village made this an ideal winter recreation, for the young and old.

Almost every family owned a sledge. Some were large, capable of carrying four, but most were two, or single seaters, or rather lyers, because most of the youngsters lay flat on their stomachs, head first, steering by their toes. The sledges were initially taken to Leaderfoot where the blacksmith, Bob Mitchell, prepared and fitted iron runners, so that speed and ease over the ice and snow was achieved. The sledges also had ropes attached for pulling.

So, when severe winter weather appeared, at night time, when there was absolutely no traffic, nearly every young person in the village enjoyed the sport. The starting, or taking off point was at the top of the steep hill by Bella Scott's shop. Some sitting upright, others lying face down, head first, all steered by their toes on the hard frozen road surface, and the momentum down hill was sufficient to allow the sledge to reach the top of the small incline at Tannachie front gate. The toe manipulations at the sharp corner required some skills, but there were few accidents.

All this took place in total darkness, there being no street lighting, consequently, those dragging sledges back to the starting point, where unable to see those descending, but the rattling of the runners on the ice, was a warning to hug the walls until the danger was past.

In winter of course darkness fell very early, so the younger boys straight from school, were among the first to get the sledges out.

On one occasion, having launched himself from the top of the hill by Bella Scott's shop, Archie Anderson encountered Jim Ford of Barnet Head farm, and his horse, at the blind corner at the foot of the village. The sledge miraculously passed beneath the legs of the horse, emerging under the wheels of the cart it was pulling at the time.

Inexplicably the horse was not brought down, nor the boy injured, but it startled both horse and Jim Ford who was naturally less than pleased.

This episode is still talked about even today when the few Newstead survivors of those days come together.

It was tremendous fun, and went on late into the night. The Anderson girls, and even my mother and her friend Mrs Forrest, had the courage enough to take part. Of course, this was long before the use of salt to disperse the ice became as popular as it is today. Not so many sledges or skaters around in Newstead today. More's the pity!

PROFILE

DUNCAN McKINNON - A LOST IMPRESARIO

Old Duncan McKinnon came down from the Oban area about 1910, recruited by Dr James Curle to assist in his first excavations of the Roman Camp at Trimontium. He resided with his wife in the top floor of the Mill Cottage, Newstead, which at that time was occupied by at least two families.

His only son Duncan, also grew up with us all in the village, but unlike his father who was of a strict Calvanistic upbringing, the son was at times unruly, often causing distress in the family. Upon leaving school at Melrose he started work as a junior apprentice clerk in the solicitor's office of Curle, Muir and Company in the Market Square, Melrose.

When war broke out in 1939, young Duncan enlisted in the 6th Bn KOSB, and was wounded, first by a German landmine dropped on the battalion near Epping, and a second time in Normandy during the invasion.

On demobilisation he returned for a short time to his previous employment, but gave it up for some unknown reason, and initially as a pastime, organised Saturday night dances in the principal Border towns.

At that time dances were the most popular Saturday night entertainment for young people, and McKinnon booked halls in almost all the Border towns, at first on a small scale, but eventually extending to a much larger audience, with dances running in four or five towns on the same evening Hawick, Galashiels, Melrose, Kelso, Lauder, Selkirk, Eyemouth, Berwick, Newton Grange, Lanark and Oban were some of the venues, but the largest hall engaged by Duncan was in Carlisle.

The problem of controlling, and staffing so many events running concurrently, and finding honest door keepers was a constant worry, but he continued to persevere. At Carlisle he succeeded in bringing big bands and entertainers, then virtually unknown, who later achieved great fame in the entertainment world. The big bands included Ted Heath, Joe Loss, Doctor Crock and his Crackpots, Joe Donnelly, Eric Winton and His Band, Eric Delanay, Lulu and the Lovers, George Melly and Acker Bilk. The Beatles, before they became famous also appeared for Duncan, as well as Jack Daniels, The Who, The Animals and the Scottish bands of Jimmy Shand, Ian Powrie and Bobby McLeod. This astonishing list of talent included famous individuals such as Denis Lotis, Dickie Valentine and Lita Rosa, all given their opportunity by Duncan. Lita Rosa singing "Walking Back to Happiness" remains an enchanting and lingering memory.

Duncan had by this time acquired a fondness for alcoholic beverages, and there were many unfortunate but amusing occasions. George Melly in his memoirs tells of a time in Carlisle, when Duncan, a bit unsteady, advanced to the front of the stage for the introduction, misjudged the distance, and ended up face down on the dance floor below, complete with dusty dinner jacket.

In a recent radio documentary, Paul McCartney related memories of the first Beatles tour under Duncan's supervision, when Paul was still studying for his 'A' levels, and his band were backing a rising star called Johnnie Gentle. Memories of the tour relate to gigs in Fraserburgh, Keith and Peterhead, where according to Paul, the Beatles were paid peanuts, and fed on tea by friendly landladies to prevent them from starving. Paul describes Duncan as a part-time Musical Agent, and a pig farmer. While Duncan did keep a few pigs when he moved to Drygrange, he is undeserving of the description of pig farmer. He claims that Duncan would turn up at concerts still bearing the aroma of the farmyard, wearing an ancient crombie coat and wellingtons.

He apparently complained to Larry Parnes, their manager, that the Beatles were too scruffy for top notch venues on their North of Scotland tour.

For a variety of reasons and despite his obvious genius and perception in this particular field, Duncan's star continued to wane, and all the endeavours of this remarkable Newstead contemporary came to an end.

It is a fitting tribute to the esteem and feelings of the entertainment world that Acker Bilk and his friends raised money for Duncan's gravestone, where he now rests in the Wairds Cemetery at Melrose.

SANTOS CASANI

Writing of Duncan McKinnon's activities brought to mind my own brief encounter with the entertainment fraternity.

When I was very young, and before television was in general use, I would listen on a crackling old wireless to a programme by a jazz pianist called Charlie Kunz, direct from the Casani Club in London.

Many years later in 1946, I was stationed in Delhi, India, with my Regiment. Santos Casani, the London club owner had joined the armed forces entertainment service, been promoted to Lt. Colonel and was now stationed in Delhi and responsible for promoting shows for the troops. Casani was a south African of Italian descent, very short in stature, but a very strongly built man, ex-wrestler and ballroom dancing champion, etc.

The authorities wished to transfer him away from Delhi GHQ to a post in the South of India, much to his dislike. He therefore feigned sickness and was admitted to the British General Hospital in Delhi Cantonment. He took with him a pistol which he kept under his pillow.

After some time it became apparent to the hospital staff that he was not really ill and the Commanding Officer of the BGH himself a Lt. Colonel ordered Casani to leave the hospital. He became angry and aggressive, refused to go, then threatened to shoot the Commanding Officer.

My regiment, stationed near the hospital, was requested to provide assistance in the decision to arrest Casani. Being at that time, big and strong, my Commanding Officer chose me for the confrontation, and together with a force of ten soldiers I proceeded to the hospital grounds and surrounded the verandah ward where Casani lay in bed.

The CO of the hospital then arrived and addressed Casani saying "Colonel Casani, you are under arrest"! Casani replied "I can't hear you!", claiming he was deaf. However after a little while he relented and saw the game was up.

We put him into the rear of a three tonne truck where I joined him and we proceeded to our Officer's Mess where he was handed over to my Commanding Officer.

In the Army, when officers are under arrest, they must be escorted at all times by two officers of equivalent rank, so two Lt. Colonels soon arrived and Casani departed. Nothing more was heard of him.

This episode, however compelled me to revise my opinion of those in the entertainment profession, although I have never forgotten "Charlie Kunz from the Casani Club, London".

THE BLOODY ORKNEYS

Having donated some of the prime and best years to serving Her Majesty, I have a sympathetic feeling for this soldier's views on a posting to the Orkneys.

This bloody Town's a bloody curse,
no bloody trains, no bloody bus,
and no one cares for bloody us
in bloody Orkney

❖　　❖　　❖

The bloody roads are bloody bad,
the bloody folks are bloody mad,
they'd make the brightest bloody sad
in bloody Orkney.

❖　　❖　　❖

All bloody clouds and bloody rains,
no bloody kerbs, no bloody drains,
the Council' got no bloody brains
in bloody Orkney.

❖　　❖　　❖

Everythings so bloody dear,
A bloody bob for bloody beer,
and is it good? no bloody fear
in bloody Orkney

❖　　❖　　❖

The bloody flicks are bloody old,
the bloody seats are bloody cold,
you can't get in for bloody gold
in bloody Orkney.

The bloody dances make you smile,
the bloody band is bloody vile,
it only cramps your bloody style
in bloody Orkney.

No bloody sport no bloody games,
no bloody fun, the bloody dames
won't even give their bloody names
in bloody Orkney.

Best bloody place is bloody bed,
with bloody ice on bloody head,
you might as well be bloody dead
in bloody Orkney.

MILLMOUNT FARM

For some reason Millmount Farm was never considered to be part of Newstead village. It is of course outside the environs of the village, but although as boys we had free access to everywhere else, Millmount was never popular, except at harvest time when rabbits were the exciting attraction.

The farm was owned by the Curle family, as it is today. Mr Purves was the tenant in the 1920's, and the land being flat was relatively easy to farm. The land extended from Newstead in the east right up to Melrose, bounded on the north by the River Tweed and the south by the Middle Walk.

One outstanding feature were the ancient trees, which started at the Newstead end of the Annay Road and continued up to Melrose where the long row of massive Beeches stood. The Middle Walk also was lined by Beech trees and in fact all the various field boundary hedges were tree lined. Only a few of the Chestnut trees remain today, and all the great Beeches are gone.

Another feature of the farm was that cattle shelters straddled the field boundaries, so that they accommodated stock from both sides, and both fields. Sadly, they have all gone now, as have most of the hedges.

The old thatched cottage by the Tweed, was occupied by the ploughman Sandy Ross. The plough of course was horse drawn. Sandy had a long grey beard and was a canny soul.

Another farm worker, old Moffat lived at Saugh Cottage in the village, which was also owned by the Curle family. He was either a bachelor or a widower, because he had a housekeeper who lived in. He was considered to be very mean, and soup seemed to be the staple diet. On one occasion the soup which had lasted for four or five days became sour and the housekeeper threw it out. When Moffat asked for his soup, and was told what had happened he became very annoyed and was overheard to say "A' could 'hae suppit them"!

In 1936, Millmount Farm was selected as the site for the Royal Highland Show. This was before the permanent Ingliston Edinburgh base for the Show was decided. The Highland Show took about six months to prepare, and hundreds of workmen lodged in the area. Wooden stands, stalls for animals and exhibits of all kinds extended from Newstead to Melrose and encompassed the entire farm area.

The workforce was considerable and nearly every house in the neighbourhood had lodgers, for nearly nine months of that year, as it took a considerable time to erect and dismantle the temporary buildings and marquees.

There was much more water in the Tweed in those days, and the farm lands barely above the water level, so that during the Autumn and Winter the Annay Road was very often flooded, and Millmount Farm completely surrounded by water for days on end.

It was thought by the old people that the river at one time, passed between the Farm house and Sandy Ross's cottage necessitating the building of the Battery Wall.

One particular incident I remember of Millmount was during a harvest. Rabbits were a plague, and cornfields abounded, so as the reaper working from the outside gradually reduced the standing corn, the rabbits were driven inwards, before deciding to make a dash for the safety of the hedgerows. Many didn't make it. On this occasion, when the cutting finished, a large rabbit hole was exposed, and Willie Anderson, hoping to find a rabbit's refuge, lay down and put his hand and arm in, only to withdraw it swiftly with a large rat hanging onto his finger.

There is a photograph in Newstead Village Hall of Sandy Ross and his horses ploughing, taken many years ago.

THE LODGE OF ST JOHN THE EVANGELIST

This painting shows Robert Mein's house in St John's Wynd, Newstead as it was in 1891. The work was commissioned by the Masonic Lodge of Melrose and executed by the local artist Willie Heatlie who lived in St John's Cottage. Historically it was the site and birth place of the very first Masonic Movement in Scotland, and is thought to have stood for over 280 years.

Andrew Mein was the writer of the first recorded Minutes of the Masonic Lodge in 1674, but it is thought that they were active long before that time. He is described as, *"Andro Mein, Meason, Portioner of Neusteid"*. During the levelling of Melrose Abbey grounds, a tombstone was uncovered belonging to ***"Andro Mein Neusteid Decessit Feb 1624 Aged 63 years"***, so we are taken back to the sixteenth century and 1561. This man therefore, may have been the father of the Robert Mein who built the house at Newstead in 1613.

Although their origins are obscure there is a suggestion that the Meins were descendants of the architect Petrus De Main. This man was employed by Robert the Bruce in rebuilding the Abbey at Melrose, following its destruction by the English in 1322. They were certainly a numerous family, principally associated with the craft of building and masonry, but embracing various other styles and occupations. They were granted lands at Newstead by James VI in 1606. The Boundary Chapter of Newstead granted in 1564, included names such as Richard Meyne, William Meyne Senior, David Meyne, Robert Meyne, William Meyne Junior and Dand Meyne. 'Dand' was the abbreviation for Andrew.

The establishment of the Newstead Masonic movement is uncertain as the written records do not go further back than 1674, but the name Mein features strongly from 1680 to 1742, the last year that the Newstead house was used as a meeting place. The Minutes were invariably written by a member of the Mein family.

An important feature of this history lies in what is described as the, "Mutual agriement betwixt the Maisonnes of the Lodge of Melros". The date of this document is 1675 and it is written by "Andro Mein, Portioner, Newsteid". This agreement is interesting as it is centred on the Masons and their apprentices. The Master Masons were unhappy that the existing term of apprenticeship, which seems to have varied between three and four years, was insufficient and detrimental to the trade, in that young men were insufficiently skilled in their craft. It had therefore been decided by the interested parties that in future, apprentice masons should be required to serve seven years. The agreement was to bind and oblige employers, and Master Masons to a uniform structure. The penalty for breaking this rule was to be twenty pounds (Scots) for each year of transgression. This document was signed by over eighty members.

It is however revealing that twenty nine who signed were Meins, and fifteen bore the name of Bunye, Bunzie, Bunnye or Bunnyie. Others were unusual such as, Robert Gollater, John Paux, Joseph Oumser, John Reink, John Couniye and Radnor Bunnye, which suggest a probable continental connection.

Some appended their Mason's marks. These were specific individual marks made upon each stone processed by a working Mason, to ensure recognition and therefore ultimate payment.

Others added their trade or profession, revealing weavers, maltmen, vintners and hostlers. So, not all the signatures were Masons, and perhaps a speculative element was involved.

This document provided a landmark in working practices at that time. The old Lodge Minutes are fascinating and revealing in the language, spelling and presentation. They embrace a range of items concerning Lodge workings, discipline, benevolent and charitable considerations. Also accounts and records of funds collected at meetings and expenditure on items necessarily incurred during the Feast of Good Saint John, which was held annually.

Today the members of the Melrose Masonic Lodge, still keep this festival when they have a torch lit procession through the town of Melrose to the ruins of the old Abbey. The Brethren afterwards dining together. The first mention of this ceremony, and its preparations appears in a Minute dated December 28th 1685 and reads:

"Given out to John Mein Ostler, upon ye Forsd day of December for meat and drink and making readie, 11 pounds, 0 shillings and 10 pence".

Another resolution passed and signed "At Newsteid the 27 day of December 1695" enacts and ordains that the "Meason Tread" and followers of the craft could not be received into the company unless they had gloves. These were to be four shillings a pair for apprentices, and five shillings for "Fallow Crafte".

Minuted on St John's day 1698, there is an account of the expenditure and money disbursed as follows:

ANDRO MEIN BRIDGEND FOR FLESH	4 pounds, 4 shillings
TO THE SAID ANDRO FOR A TICKET	10 shillings
TO JOHN MEIN FOR TWO SHEETS OF PAPER	6 pence
TO JAMES BUNYE FOR KEEPING THE KEY	14 shillings
TO JAMES BUNYE FOR GOING TO MELROSE	3 shillings
ABOUT THE FLESH AND BREAD	
TO AGNES PHILP FOR AILE	6 pounds 13 shillings
TO AGNES PHILP FOR MAKING THE MEAT	1 pound 15 shillings
READY AND ALSO FOR BEARE	
TO WILLIAM BROWN FOR WHYT BREAD	2 pounds 5 shillings and sixpence
FOR TWO LEGS OF MUTTON AND AN	2 pounds 3 shillings and
PUND TOBACO AND PIPS	ten pence
FOR AN CAPFUL OF SALT	3 shillings

An interesting entry, on the 27th December 1698 states *"The forsd day ther was full pour given to John Mein Tounheid and John Mein Wynd to put the bonds in execution against the First of March 1699 for buying the Mort cloth"*. The Mort cloth referred to was a velvet pall spread over a coffin and used during funerals. The Mort cloth was solely for use at Mason's funerals and other members of the Brethren's families. The rules were restrictive, each member was allowed to make use of it, his eldest son if under 21 years of age, but other sons exceeding that age if going to a trade other than Masons, were excluded. The daughters until marriage, and if married to a member, also had a right, as had his spouse, a members widow, until she remarried, but no person not a member had any right to a Mort cloth.

However, charges were made for the service of the Mort cloth. An item in the Records states: *"That the officer must go along with the Mortcloth and take charge thereof for which he shall receive from the person employing him, one shilling sterling if within six miles of Melrose, but if above six and not exceeding twenty miles, two shillings sterling"*.

An example of the benevolence of the Masonic movement is disclosed in a Minute of 25 September 1813, *"The French Brethren of the Lodge of St John under the distinctive appellation of benevolence constituted by the French prisoners of war on parole were invited to attend"*. In the archives is a document of the names of the French prisoners, given as an expression of their appreciation of the kindness received during their sojourn in Melrose.

It seems that the old Masonic Brethren rigorously enforced their Bye-Laws, as the following extract reveals, dated Newstead February 2nd 1741:

"The Company has enacted that the said James Wallace Mason in Melrose and Andrew Bunyie Mason in Newstead that each of them is to pay one shilling sterling for not compearing with their gloves at the time of the Company's meetings before 12 a clock and that one shilling sterling they must pay immediately in with their gloves as witness our description day and date designed above".

The old Minutes are fascinating, and one on 27th December 1688 states *"recivied fra Mungo Park, nin pund sixteen shilin scotes"*. So,

Newstead lays claim to the Masonic birthplace, though but little of it is to be seen today.

The reference to Mungo Park, recalls the story that when after many long years in darkest Africa, he was returning on a short visit to his home and birthplace at Foulshiels in the Yarrow Valley. His aged parents however were unaware of his home coming, but his old mother being awake early on a dark morning, and on hearing approaching footsteps on the hard metalled road, was heard to say with a sigh, "Aye, that will be Mungo"!

Some time therefore between 1741 and 1744 the Masons abandoned the Newstead connection, when the Lodge in Melrose became the Masonic centre. Mein's house therefore was occupied continuously until prior to its demolition in 1892. Upon its demolition in 1892 the ornamental carved window above the door, was preserved and removed by the Masons of Melrose to their Lodge.

When the Lodge of St John moved to Melrose it seems that its Newstead origins and connections were largely forgotten, understandably perhaps, as nothing remained or was visible of the main building other than a small insignificant remnant of a wall.

All that remains of the old Lodge today.

However, when in recent years it was decided to hold an Annual Melrose Festival, the Masonic movement was encouraged to become incorporated in the ceremonial functions. So annually, the Brothers of the Lodge of St John the Evangelist, attend at the site of Robert Mein's house in St John's Wynd Newstead to pay their tribute.

It seems fitting that the Commemorative plaque on the remnants, was donated by another old native of the village, Willie Cleaver, now residing in America.

So, the Newstead colony of Masons left an indelible mark of their presence in this ancient and historic old village.

NEWSTEAD'S TOWNHEAD FARM

When I grew up in Newstead, Riddell had superseded Brydon at Townhead. The 'CB1897' in the stone work over the old creamery door, marked the intention that Brydon's occupancy should not be forgotten.

Today, the creamery is a listed building. The farm probably has an ancient history and may have evolved like so much of old Newstead in the fashion prevailing then, when organised planning was unheard of. This resulted in the old farm house, and the farm lands all being on the south side of the roadway, whilst the main steading, always referred to as the 'stackyard', stables, byres and storage barns, were situated on the north side, so animals and farm machinery had, of necessity, to cross the main road.

Long columns of cows in single file crossing twice daily, from their grazing fields for milking in the byres, and in the process depositing much mud and other unsavoury residue, had to be accepted. The cows usually came via the road under the Railway Bridge, at the east end of the village, which was continually wet and which became known locally as 'The Mucky Brig' . The peculiar gait and treading of the cows, left an unusual corrugated pattern on the soft surface, never seen today. The small eighty acres of land extended from south of the railway, up to the line of the Bogley Burn road, in a series of very small fields, enclosed by numerous hawthorn hedges.

Apart from grazing pastures, the crops included, corn, hay, turnips etc. Irish transient labourers assisted when turnips had to be singled. All done by hand and hoe. A service road ran parallel to the Railway line and was bounded on the south by a very high, uncut hawthorn hedge. Both the road and the hedges have gone forever.

When at the ripening of the harvest and before the cutting by binder could begin, men with scythes cut the entrance and also an area around the inside of the field. The machine could then be introduced with no wasteful damage to the crop. Local labour was recruited to stack the corn sheaves, in groups of eight to assist the ripening.

However, the final gathering in for stacking and ultimate threshing in the autumn, required heavy fork work, so female workers were confined to the initial process of gathering sheaves, and 'stooking' as it was commonly known.

The refreshments provided in the harvest fields, which I remember so well, was cold water, in a large milk churn, to which several handsfull of oatmeal had been added. The meal rested on the bottom, and the whole assumed a milky appearance, but was refreshing and unusual, but a frugal provision for thirsty workers.

So the cows produced much milk, and there being no door-step deliveries then, villagers requiring a supply were compelled to journey to the farm with jugs or pitchers. With no exact measurement available, the amount supplied, and the price to be charged, became open to debate. In due course, Riddell became more adventurous, and with a small pony and trap containing a milk churn with a tap fixed to control the flow, the sons toured the village.

Accurate measuring was still not in vogue and the health authorities also were unhappy with hygiene at the cooling and creamery activities. So the local milk industry gradually evolved.

This gradually developed and eventually embraced Melrose and Dingleton. Milk deliveries to Dingleton were generally made in the evening, after the milking. On some occasions the milkman being familiar entered the house. On one such occasion when the household was at tea, and not being unobservant, he was heard to remark "eggs for your tea tonight again! How can you afford it?"

There is so much to be written about the farm. Its central position meant that most activities were under observation, and the various animals were an attraction for many of the children. Personally, I enjoyed many happy moments and have lots of memories.

In 1922, the large hay barns were destroyed by fire, late at night, the blaze lightening up the sky in spectacular fashion. The Melrose Fire Brigade was called out and the burn on the Back Road entrance, not piped then, was dammed with sand bags to provide a water supply. The antiquated machine was drawn by a horse, and the pumping required four men on each side, raising and lowering two wooden pumping handles which ran the length of the fire engine on both sides. The scarcity of water and the distance to the stackyard meant that the firemen's efforts were ineffective, and two barns of hay were completely destroyed.

Many years later, a local boy arsonist, set fire to, and destroyed the new hay sheds built as replacements. An unsavoury feature of the stack yard was the enormous enclosed dung heap at the main gate, and although this was emptied and cleared away periodically, the flies attracted, and the smell produced, detracted somewhat from a potential for rural charm. However, it was not unattractive to my dear mother's pet tortoise, which every year, at a certain part of the season, headed determinedly for the heat generated by decaying matter. There being little traffic the tortoise was often rescued from the road way. Certainly Townhead Farm, exposed as it was, was a definite feature of the village, in those days.

PROFILE: WAT TAIT

LUNATIC LANE

Wat Tait lived in the last house on the right at the top of St John's Wynd. It was really a Butt and Ben, very dark inside, with small windows. It was the scene of a tragedy, when after Wat died, the later occupants, two elderly people, were found dead from gas poisoning. It then became a broiler house for chickens, owned by Barnethead Farm. It has since been levelled, and is gone for ever.

The photograph shows Wat Tait's house at the top of St John's Wynd. Plain Tree Cottage and the Plain Tree are at the top right. Note the road surface.

Wat had three sons, but I do not remember a wife, so perhaps he was a widower. He was employed as a railway surfaceman, smoked a pipe continuously, and his daily ritual on his way to work was to call in to Bella Scott's shop (now Drewen Cottage) for a supply of tobacco and matches.

He lived alone, as all his three sons lodged in Melrose Lunatic Asylum. There being no indoor water supply, he drew water from the old pump well in the corner of the house opposite, and he always looked unwashed.

The Lunatic Asylum, now Dingleton Hospital, had a large number of patients, and was always full, although naturally, not all were from the Melrose area. It is debatable if this reflected the attitude of the medical profession in those days, because certification of so many would be unacceptable today.

The Asylum then, had a large number of inmates, including the three Tait brothers, and they were referred to as patients. Correspondingly there was a large staff of warders, not nurses, as the male patients were employed as gardeners, to occupy their time in the extensive gardens.

Some of the less violent patients were allowed out to walk down to Melrose town. It was common to meet them on Dingleton Brae and although not all wore distinctive clothes, it was a simple conjecture to identify a patient from the Asylum.

However, there were frequent attacks by inmates on unsuspecting staff, and despite being surrounded by a high stone wall, there were often escapes. The Taits often escaped, and naturally, headed for Newstead and home, hiding in the bushes, hoping to see their father on his return from work. They were of course often observed, and reported to the hospital, recaptured and returned before this could take place. A pathetic situation.

Young Wat however possessed a certain cunning. During one escape attempt he was quickly spotted and a chase began as he ran down Chief's Wood Road from the Asylum, heading towards Darnick Vale, hotly pursued by warders wearing white coats. This was observed by some pedestrians at Darnick, who rushed out to bar his way and make an interception. As Wat approached, he called out "Get out of the way, it's a race, it's a race!", and the bemused group stood aside and let him pass.

Another of his past-times was photography. The wooded area near the Asylum, at Bowden Moor was known to the locals as the Duke's Woods, and was a popular rendezvous for courting couples. Wat was known to frequent the area, and take snapshots of couples in compromising situations. He developed the photos and found a ready sale, when he was allowed to go down to Melrose township.

However, it seems he didn't have access to proper developing materials, and after a time the images faded or disappeared completely. One customer whose purchased photograph disappeared, accosted Wat on Dingleton Brae and said "Do you remember the photo you sold me?" when Wat replied "yes", he said "Well it has disappeared". Wat then asked him how much he had paid for it, "Six pence", he said, so Wat retorted "well that's disappeared too".

This eccentric attitude however was not entirely confined to the children. Old Wat, although never thought to be a drinker, often cycled into Melrose in the evenings. One night on his return, he encountered one of the few motor cars on the roads then, and sustained a broken nose. When asked by some neighbours, what exactly had happened, he told them that he thought the approaching lights were of two bicycles, and he decided to drive between them.

Typical Marx brothers stuff if it weren't indeed true. There is nothing like this in Newstead today.

NEWSTEAD HOSPITAL

In 1901, the erection of a Joint Infectious Diseases Hospital at Newstead was under discussion, so it is likely that the hospital was actually built in 1903 or 1904. The present day Rushbank Housing Estate was, I remember, green agricultural land farmed by Jim Ford of Barnet Head, so the hospital site was probably the same.

In any event, in my time, the hospital was a going concern, greatly admired and appreciated by the villagers, and something of a showpiece. It was not at that time surrounded by trees, as it is today. The lovely old Copper Beech by the entrance being the sole adornment and the low wall, with cast iron railings, wide enough for our little feet, meant we could stand there and communicate by signs, with the patients who could be seen in beds. This I remember particularly when a Scarlet fever epidemic closed the village school, and some of our school mates had been admitted.

The hospital staff consisted of a Matron and a number of nurses, who lived in a large building by the main gate, known as the Nurses Home. There was one main building, with isolated verandahs separate at the rear, where TB patients lay in beds outside, but under cover, at all times, even during the winter.

The two local Doctors McMillan and Spiers, who lived in Melrose, presumably referred sick patients to the hospital, but I am not sure of this, as Dr. McMillan removed my tonsils at home, on our kitchen table, and on another occasion I had a broken finger stitched up without anaesthetic. Stories of similar sewings by Dr. Spiers, too drunk to even thread the needle also were common.

So the connection between our Doctors and the hospital remain obscure. The diseases most common in my recollections were Diphtheria, Smallpox, Measles and German Measles, Mumps and Tuberculosis. St Vitus Dance, unheard of today, was often a subject talked about at that time.

In addition to the nursing staff, some village males were employed as gardeners, stokers etc., and old Duncan McKinnon from Mill Cottage was one. Another, Dick Henderson, lived in the house now

Westend Cottage, with the date 1764 over the doorway. He was an Albino, with white hair and pink eyes, and during bright sunny weather had great difficulty in finding his way about.

There was of course no refuse collection system in the village, so all hospital discarded material was dumped behind the hospital on the bank, where it eventually found its way downhill towards the river Tweed. Old bandages, bottles etc., formed a considerable heap, and we always were apprehensive when passing nearby. So the hospital functioned well for many years, up to 1939 and the outbreak of the war.

By then, we boys had grown up and become aware of the more attractive members of the nursing staff. One in particular was known just as Blondie, for obvious reasons, and a delicious petite red head, who of course, turned many heads.

Circumstances changed and after the war the hospital seems to have become a mere storage area, although an ambulance operated from Newstead. The driver was Jock McKenzie, who conveyed patients to and from Peel Hospital, for treatment.

On one particular occasion, he returned to Newstead with Mrs McGinnis from Claymires Cottage, in the rear. For some reason, instead of taking her home, he drove straight to the hospital, put the ambulance in the garage, locked the door and went home for his supper. After nearly six hours, passers by heard calls for help, and the poor woman was finally rescued in a very distressed condition. So much for Jock McKenzie.

The lovely old Newstead Hospital of bygone days, still recalls fond memories for me.

NEWSTEAD'S TRANSPORT PIONEER

As a child in Newstead, I do not remember anyone in the village owning a motor car, but of course there were some to be seen. The motor transport revolution was about to descend upon us all.

Tom Bell, one of the numerous sons of John Bell the miller of Newstead Mill, was obviously a young man of vision and perception, for here we see Newstead's very first motor bus. Unfortunately, it is not now known if it was a profitable venture, for after a short time, it

Tom Bell – Bus owner.

52

was taken over by a Selkirk partnership of Brooke and Amos. Willie Amos, was from a farming family, so it would appear that neither Tom Bell, nor Willie Amos, had appreciable mechanical backgrounds.

The photograph shows Bell's bus enclosed and weather proof, a contrast to those of Brooke and Amos, which were mostly open to all weathers, with the leather hood telescoped at the rear. The bench seats reached across the vehicle, from side to side, and the Conductor, when collecting fares, stood clinging to the door handle with one hand, isolated on a walkway on the other side. He was thus able to reach the passengers without entering the vehicle itself.

This style was popular when conveying large parties, such as Newstead Picnic trips, where the children could perch on the hood in the rear. Brooke and Amos were soon also, taken over, this time by SMT, the Scottish Motor Traction Company.

As people mostly walked if they could, rather than spend what little money they had, it seems possible that Tom Bell's bus venture was not a great success.

Tom Bell, driver on right, with Charlie Mitchell as Conductor.

SUNDIALS

Life in Newstead is sheer bliss, now the traffic has switched to the by-pass.

There is now much less movement than in my youth 80 years ago. Then the traffic was generated by horse, bicycle or foot, long before the bus pioneers Brooke and Amos appeared on the scene.

I suspect it was generated by Bella Scott's general shop, "Mud" Miles' Pub, and Paterson the Fleischer's Butchery.

The three farms, and the various lodging houses reputed to have served as accommodation for Irish labourers constructing the new railway, are also likely to have been a contributory factor.

However, it is not generally known that Newstead was famous for its sundials, which used to decorate the dwellings of the masons of the old "Ludge" there.

A few still remain, but many are disappearing or failing through neglect. Some of the pedestal types were very fine indeed.

One of the best examples was to be seen over the door of Riddells' Townhead farmhouse. Above the dial was an inscription in Hebrew and Latin, reminding the reader that life is a fleeting shadow, and surmounted by a finely carved head, resembling what we might imagine Sir Walter Scott to be like in his youth.

One of the Newstead treasures at that time was the "Cradle Stone", situated on top of a derelict cottage at the foot of Main Street. On one side of its upward projections were two crossed spades, plus a bell with a hand grasping it. On the other side was an hour glass with the motto "Memento Mori-Fugit Hora", and the date 1561.

Faintly visible were words which looked like Wright, or Wight and Alexander. This stone disappeared mysteriously between the wars, although the encompassing stone framework is still visible today.

Also at this site is the sole remaining "loupin' on" stane – a relic of the horse transport then prevailing.

Foreign visitors still come enquiring about the sundials. In fact Newstead is a historian's dream.

Its more recent connections with Tom Scott, RSA, and Willie Heatley are not in the least overshadowed by Turner, whose painting of Melrose was completed from a site above "Cowies Hole", by Tweedside.

The sad thing about Newstead, however, is that newcomers are changing the ancient names of houses, paths, and lanes, and the character and charm of the village of old is slipping away forever.

HARDIES' HOUSE

This photograph shows the last of the thatched houses in the village. It is at the east end and shows part of the Stackyard wall of Townhead Farm. Library Cottage, and Tweedview are in the background.

The house was occupied in my early days by a widow, Mrs Hardie, and her son Jim who was a labourer, and often the worse for wear through drink, especially on Saturdays. Mrs Hardie was often seen sitting on the doorstep, smoking a white clay pipe. The Hardies drew water from the well in the 'Well Roadie' opposite the house.

It will be noted that the thatched roof is in a poor condition, and I remember the repairs carried out by thatchers from South of the Border. Presumably the art of thatching had been lost to the locals.

The two figures by the house are familiar in my memory and may be Jim Hardie, on the left, and Tom Mitchell on the right. The wooden lintel over the small window in the gable is clearly visible.

Yet another of the ancient village houses gone forever!

VANISHED PEOPLE

INGEN JOHNNY

The French onion sellers from Brittany were always a summer feature, in days gone by. They were obviously an enterprising lot. Boat loads of onions were brought over, and ships berthed at Leith or Musselburgh, where they remained until the entire cargo was sold.

The Frenchmen in their hooped jerseys and wearing berets, pushing their bicycles festooned with strings of onions, covered the country. They appeared everywhere, spoke broken English, often in a jocular fashion, engaging in repartee with the village housewives.

One well remembered character came for many years. His signature whistling of 'Apres La Guerre Fini', always attracted notice, particularly from the war veterans.

CALLER HERRIN'

The fishwives from Musselburgh's famous Fisher Row, arrived during the Herring season, with large quantities of fish.

They wore attractive and distinctive blue and white skirts, tucked up and caught at each side at the waist, to reveal yet another striped petticoat. They carried large square wicker baskets of Herring, which was the only type of fish they brought with them.

The baskets were extremely heavy, and as they came by train, and had to walk to the various villages, the women were mostly mature strong individuals.

Sometimes, if no sale was forthcoming at a village doorstep, they became frustrated and forceful. I believe in Musselburgh they formed a famous choir, but little or no singing in Newstead, however.

SUITCASE SALESMEN

A common feature of village life, in my time, was the travelling salesman. These men, mostly white, but later almost entirely Indian or Pakistani, would arrive unannounced, carrying one or sometimes two, suitcases, strapped up and bulging with linen goods, clothing and other types of apparel, mostly for ladies. Camisoles were one item I particularly remember.

He was permitted to enter the house, spread the goods on the floor, and neighbours would assemble, so that his wares could be examined and discussed. Frank Church, whose family owned a large clothing shop in Galashiels High Street, was a regular. It appears to have been a popular and satisfactory method of trading in those days.

The Kleeneze Brush salesmen however, were seldom received with such enthusiasm.

GUISERS

At Halloween, it was the custom, long ago in the village, for groups of children to arrive at the door, at night, announcing themselves as 'Guisers'. They were then allowed in, where some sort of playlet, which unfortunately I have long forgotten, was enacted, involving a fight where someone ends up on the floor. A boy dressed as a doctor, wearing a top hat appears, and the others chant the rhyme, "here comes in old Doctor Brown, the best old doctor in the town, a little to his nose, and a little to his toes, rise up Jack and sing a song". After a gesture to nose and toes, the one on the floor arises, and sings a song. I'm sure there was more than this, but the memory has gone. I also believe that a collection was taken.

TRAMPS

The poverty of those early times, meant that there were many tramps, both male and female, moving around the country looking for charity. Most towns had special lodging houses where they could stay for the night; if they could afford to pay, but most slept in the open.

Many appeared regularly in the local court rooms charged with begging or drunkenness, or often breaches of the peace. They seemed to have a regular travelling beat; because the same individuals turned up again and again, and became well known. Two in particular, a female known to the villagers as Berwick Nell, and an aged man Old Hardie.

The modus operandi was to call at a house in the early morning, presenting a tin can or container, and requesting some hot water to make tea. If this was seen to be forthcoming, the next move was to ask for a pinch of tea. Then a little bread, and so on until they were given enough food for a breakfast of sorts. Some villagers turned them away, so they soon realised which houses to visit, and which not.

Certainly Mrs Forrest's and my mother's kind heartedness drew regular visits.

VANISHED NAMES AND EXPRESSIONS

THE KILLIN HOOSE

This large and extensive building on the Annay Road, was especially designed and equipped for its purpose, the slaughter of animals.

The Melrose butchers each had separate slaughtering areas and performed their grisly duties with much less sophistication than in butchery today.

My first and only visit as a young and curious boy, was a disillusionment not yet forgotten.

After slaughter the intestines and other unwanted organs, were transported in a special metal cart drawn by horse, and open at the top to Hamilton's fields, on the high road between Newstead and Melrose. The contents were then spread over the fields, presumably as a form of fertiliser. The progress of this vehicle through Melrose, with its high smelling contents open and visible, was best avoided.

The decaying matter attracted many rats, and colonies so numerous, that the roots of hedges became exposed, established themselves by the main road.

THE WILDERNESS

The land now occupied by St Dunstans housing complex and the Melrose Health Centre, was in the past commonly known as 'The Wilderness'. The origin of this is obscure, but the name certainly appears on ancient documents, indicating some antiquity.

DOOKIN

During the hot summer months, the Mecca for all village youngsters was, of course, the river Tweed.

Despite the raw untreated sewage, clearly visible, this was no restriction or distraction. So nearly everyone enjoyed the 'dookin'. The deeper pools were dangerous and provided many near misses and rescues, but sadly Ikey Stuart paid the penalty by drowning in the Tweed, and only just a schoolboy.

Coupled with 'dookin' was eel stabbing. Eels abounded in the Tweed then, and rested under the many large stones and boulders in the river bed. When they were moved or lifted delicately, the head of the eel would appear out of curiosity.

The practice then was to spear the head with a fork, and old kitchen forks were favourites. If successful, the wriggling eel and fork was thrown out and on to the river bank. This was by means of a boyish sport, and the eels never for human consumption.

THE SKERRS

The erosion of the higher banks of the Tweed at Newstead, opposite Sandie Ross's cottage at Millmount, and also below the hospital, produced very high ridges where the softer soil had been washed down by rain leaving the harder base in situ. They rose from a deep base revealing abandoned rabbit holes and providing nesting sites for Jackdaws and Rock Pigeons. The earth was coloured red, and inaccessible to humans. None of these unusual features remain today, but to the locals they were the 'skerrs'.

CAIRNS

This was the common name given to the cement structures protruding into the river and designed to deflect the flow, thus restricting erosion of the river banks.

They were, of course, advantageous to fishermen, by allowing access to centre water in the river. The ancient Cairns were invariably ideally sited.

The modern, amateurish one now set above the Boiler Pool has been a disaster. The resulting eddy has, over recent years, resulted in the destruction of the entire river bank which had stood for years.

However, today, with more sophisticated affluent salmon fishers and land owners from south of the Border, has come the description Croy or Croix. So it seems Cairns are no longer Cairns!

THE DOUBLE HEDGE

This was the common term and designation of the two parallel hedges and the line of Ash trees running north and south, from the Trimontium Monument to its junction with the Broomhill Road. It formed the west boundary of the principal Roman Fort site.

Normally, fields are separated by a line of hedge or fence, but this particular one is unusual in that the hedges were at least four yards apart and wide enough for carts to pass, except that the centre contained large Ash trees. None of the Newstead ancients had an explanation for this.

THE BACK O' THE RAW

This referred to the tree lined area running north and south, and on the west side of the Yiddy road to the Tweed. It separated the high ground from the Mill dam, and the lower ground was water logged, swampy and a haven for many frogs and newts.

In addition was a large cave, underneath supported by the roots of a tree at the top of the bank. It was extremely popular with the village boys as a play area. The first small Newstead sewage system was also sited nearby.

Understandably after so many hundreds of years, the ancient trees are succumbing to age, winds and weather and the 'raw' is unsightly today.

THE BULLERS

The origin of this name is obscure, but it is preserved in many older maps of the Newstead area. It refers to a stretch of land in the vicinity of the stone depot, north east of the Newstead Hospital and continuing along the higher land along Tweedside.

THE ABBEY HOTEL

This photograph shows a corner of the Abbey Hotel, Melrose, long since demolished, and the thatched cottage which shared a joint entrance to Melrose Abbey and the Hotel. The present entrance and ticket office to the Abbey occupies the site today.

The workmen are engaged in its removal. The characters from left to right are: *Jim Whitworth, Jock Pringle, Dod Brown,* and *Jim Scott* is sitting on the 'Loupin' on stane'. Centre beside the horse is *Geordie Todd* the farmer, Mrs Hamilton wife of the proprietor, and three female hotel staff. Behind the girls, in uniform, is the Melrose Abbey curator at that time. on the ladder at the bottom is *Harold Hall*. The person on the thatch at the left, and in white shirt sleeves, is *Mr Frater*.

Harold Hall was an ex Royal Navy diver. I remember him at work in the Tweed, reinforcing the old Leaderfoot road bridge.

Dod Brown, with hammer and white apron round his middle was a joiner, who doubled also as caretaker at the Corn Exchange, where he had accommodation and lived.

One winter's night, during a concert in the hall, the central heating pipes burst. Dod Brown, in order to stem the flow, dashed to the ladies cloakroom, grabbed some coats, and stuffed them into the pipes. Jock Pringle's wife was particularly irate and upset that her one and only best coat was ruined!

Unfortunately we have no date for the photograph, only that it was taken on the 3rd of September, but it is all within contemporary memory and the individuals well remembered.

The "Loupin' on Stane", for the uninitiated was to enable horses to be mounted without further assistance. Only one such stone exists in Newstead village today.

Many newcomers to Melrose, or younger residents today, will no doubt be surprised to know that in my younger days, the main entrance to the Abbey was bounded on the north side by a large thatched dwelling house and the then Abbey Hotel. It is even more astonishing to think that it was built within the old Abbey grounds. It was then owned by the Hamilton family.

The Hotel was a substantial, three storey building as part of it can be seen in the accompanying photograph. It was most likely originally a coaching Inn. Certainly the stage and mail coaches operated from a collecting point in the adjacent Abbey Street. The Melrose Abbey area at that time is difficult to visualise today, with its many new roads and housing layouts.

Buccleuch Street at that time was not completely straight either and its junction with Abbey Street terminated in an 'S' bend. A large dwelling house occupied by the Kidd family, including a garden and a large pear tree, stood in the area now the Abbey car park. Also, that particular part of the east end of Buccleuch Street, and where the small isolated cafe is today, was occupied by Johnny Wood's grocers shop. Across the road was Gibson's saddlery, presumably dependant to some extent on the Hamilton's for the Hotels coaches and horses business.

Today Morrow Gardens housing and the present ornamental gardens have replaced what then contained a huge conglomeration of stables, pends, and sheds for the various horse drawn carriages.

The solitary horse drawn hearse in Melrose was also housed there. The structures were mostly of wood with corrugated roofing, unsightly, unattractive to the eye and ill painted in a variety of colours. This establishment held the coaches required by the Abbey Hotel guests who were met at Melrose Station on arrival and driven in style.

I remember at least three cab drivers, Willie Duff, Jamie Gordon and Joe Snowie, who were always suitably dressed with top hats and long whips of white cord. Top hats were known locally as 'tile' hats. The George and Abbotsford hotel was also owned by the Hamilton family, so the horse transport monopoly seems to have remained in their control.

The thatched house by the entrance to Melrose Abbey, shown in the photograph was taken down long before the last war, but the hotel itself remained into the early fifties. The various outhouses and coach accommodation disappeared also at that time.

The last proprietor was Jock Hamilton, referred to elsewhere. He was a jovial, generous, extrovert, fond of practical jokes and extremely popular and well known in the town and surrounding areas. So his general 'Bon Homie' style induced a varied clientele at the Hotel bar, and it became by reputation, a regular attraction for many, who were not necessarily affluent, customers. He was short of stature, extremely fat and latterly almost unable to walk because of his excess weight. Nevertheless Jock was a 'character' in true style, and a type not seen around today.

My earliest recollection of the Abbey Hotel was when at the age of four or five, King George V and Queen Mary paid a visit to Melrose Abbey, and we as school infants, each issued with a paper Union Jack flag, were marshalled at the Abbey entrance to cheer a welcome.

Prominent on a table on the hotel mid staircase, stood a large glass phial containing a snake, preserved in alcohol. This was an exceptionally large specimen of an adder, which had been found on the Eildon Hills amid great publicity. Jock Hamilton acquired it and it became the focus of much interest among the locals and hotel residents alike. However, the alcoholic aspect proved too much for some of the hotel servants. At the time it was suspected that an Irish chamber maid had succumbed to temptation when the container was discovered one day to be drained of its contents. The individual however apparently suffered no ill effects, settling, after marriage in Melrose, and finally being a 'character' in the village of Newstead.

Jock Hamilton and my father were on very friendly terms, so during the final Hotel closure and disposal of surplus merchandise, we became reluctant recipients of large amounts of wine from the cellars. My father was completely tee-total, but our friends certainly benefited. Much more acceptable was the Hamilton families' African Grey Parrot. However, it soon became apparent that it possessed an unhappy vicious streak to its nature, being aggressive to all except my mother who seemed to be able to handle it with ease.

The only remaining traces of the Hotel to be seen today are in the sunken indentations near the ticket office and entrance to the Abbey itself. Many of the local ancients however still retain happy memories of the Old Abbey Hotel.

WORTHIES

In days gone by, in villages and enclosed communities, when television and such artificial forms of entertainment were unknown, there often existed many apparently eccentric individuals. Their extraordinary, unsociable often lunatic, but mostly humorous behaviour, became a source of enjoyable amusement to many, and so they acquired a certain notoriety, as "worthies" or "characters".

They were in abundance in Newstead and Melrose when I was young.

Here are a few:

JOCKIE DICKSON

Jockie Dickson lived with his wife, in a small house now demolished, behind today's Drewen Cottage. The entrance was by a narrow lane which still exists. Jockie was often drunk, especially on a Saturday, which was pay day, and turning up regularly in a paralytic condition without much money, did not please Mrs Dickson. So, there were frequent rows, with much shouting and Jockie threatening to commit suicide.

On one such difficult day, in exasperation, and intending to frighten his wife, Jockie emerged from the house, stood in the middle of the road and shouted in a loud voice to passers by "Can you show me the road to the Tweed?"! He was of course quite well aware of where the river Tweed ran.

It is doubtful if Mrs Dickson was impressed, she had probably heard it before.

JOCK PRINGLE

Jock Pringle, was a scion of an old Newstead family of Masons, who built amongst others, Hawthorn Cottage in the Back Road, and also Claymires Cottage. Jock, himself a mason was employed by Spiers, the Melrose builders and often did restoration work on Melrose Abbey. He was a tall, thin rangy type, with little or no malice and a pleasant sense of humour.

An expert fisherman, Jock was able to catch fish when others were less successful, but his spare time was mostly taken up in poaching. Salmon were in abundance in the Tweed in those days, and the fields alive with rabbits, pheasants, pigeons and other game, so there was plenty of activity.

Old Tom Mitchell, of St John's Cottage, was his particular poaching crony. Both carried shotguns, and appeared to have free range over the nearby farm fields, but they resented any opposition.

Many of the village cats which strayed afar hunting rabbits, simply disappeared. A common ploy was to throw the dead cat into the road, which suggested that it had been struck by a passing vehicle.

The Ship Inn at Melrose was Jock's main outlet for salmon he had poached. Jock's particular vice however, was a fondness for drink, and invariably each Saturday he arrived at Newstead with his bicycle, on his way home to Hawthorn Cottage, very much to quote Burns' Tam O' Shanter "glorious oer all the ills of life victorious!".

Being unable to cycle up the hills in the village, in his condition, and in order to sober up before reaching home, he would stop and call in to his sister, Mrs Forrest at Eildon View, then proceed to our house, where my mother had to cope with hours of garrulous talk.

A sure sign was to see the bicycle lying in the middle of the roadway. After a while he would decide to make for home, via the right of way known as the Well Roadie, which crossed the burn by a narrow stone bridge, and rose steeply to the Back Road.

For some reason, Jock always mounted his bike, wobbling down the narrow track to the bridge, misjudging and ending up in the burn. This was always highly amusing to us boys, but not so to his wife, a fierce Irish woman viewing the spectacle from the Back Road.

I have mentioned in the 'Fur and Feather' story of how Jock released a ferret one Saturday, in Mrs Forrest's house, to annoy her pet cat. She was very house proud, and kept the hall way linoleum highly polished. One day when the front door was open, Jock, on passing by, picked up a handful of gravel and threw it into the passage way, supposedly for fun.

On an other occasion, when returning in darkness from a salmon poaching trip to the Tweed near Leaderfoot, he took a short cut, and on stepping over the low wall of the stone depot near the hospital, stepped onto the back of a large bear, whose German master was asleep by its side. Fortunately for Jock the bear was muzzled at the time. There are many such tales to remind us of Jock Pringle, however, it was he who finally destroyed the lovely old Domed Well in the Well Roadie, to get bricks to build a house for his ferrets.

It is true, the well by then had been superseded by a proper piped water system in the village, and was no longer in use, but it was a very fine example, its unusual style being very shallow, with no pumping mechanism and easy access to water.

JOCK HAMILTON

Although not a Newstead native, Jock was well known in the village. He was one of the Hamilton family who owned the Abbey, and George and Abbotsford hotels in Melrose, and extensive lands in Newstead, bordering the west side of the Banks Road leading from Newstead to the Bogley Burn. Riddell's Townhead farm extended to only eighty acres, so to make it viable, they rented extra fields from the Hamiltons.

Jock was a true character, being very, very fat and with a great sense of fun. During the summer he recruited lots of Newstead and Melrose boys, to collect seagulls eggs at Bemersyde Moss. This was a large swampy area of bog, interspersed with tufts of grass and rushes, which for many years had been a breeding ground for Black Headed Gulls, being safe from most predators.

We were driven there by Jock, in an open tourer, and the eggs collected in baskets, later to be dispatched the same night from Melrose Station, by the Pullman en route for the London hotels and markets, masquerading as Plovers eggs. The Black Headed Gulls known to the locals as 'Pickie Maws', were of course far removed from Plovers.

Looking back, I have thought at what stage of freshness, or incubation, the eggs were, because every egg to be seen was gathered, and there was no way of knowing if chicks were about to hatch or not.

One day, one of the party, Jimmy Allen, who lived at the East Port in Melrose, missed his footing and fell into some water. In order to dry his clothes and himself in the sun, he stripped of completely only to find he was under observation from high ground above, the audience mostly curious farm children.

Always full of humour, Jimmy looked up at them and shouted out "It's Robinson Crusoe you buggers!" at which they immediately disappeared over the hill.

For us, as young boys, it was all great fun and enjoyable, and we were always eager to take part in what was really a unique exciting adventure. I can't remember ever being paid, or if payment was offered, but Willie Cleaver, now in California has told me that Jock offered an inducement of threepence at the time, but it was never forthcoming, and Willie was too scared to ask again.

Today the same Bemersyde Moss has an abundance of breeding black headed Gulls. It is owned by Earl Haig. Although under the Wildlife and Country Act 1981, all birds and their eggs are protected, the gamekeeper collects 10,000 eggs annually under licence. The eggs provide a revenue for the estate and are, as in Jock Hamilton's day, sold to the London markets, as 'Plovers' eggs, a gourmet food.

Jock Hamilton had a glorious sense of the absurd, and revelled in inducing people, either in his bar at the Abbey Hotel, or elsewhere, to indulge in foolish or outrageous behaviour, to the amusement of himself and others. Apparently innocent, unintended situations or actions by Jock were designed to entrap the unwary, resulting in many humorous, funny and deflating experiences. Serving one hundred per cent proof whisky or encouraging customers to inebriation by providing free beer for all, at his expense, had the aim of producing absurd behaviour and amusement. He was renowned as a jovial landlord at the Melrose Abbey Hotel.

On one particular Sunday morning Mr Frater, who lived in Dingleton, came down hill, in his carpet slippers, hoping to collect his Sunday papers. He encountered Jock Hamilton driving in his large Sunbeam motor car, and was invited into the car for a sightseeing tour of the town. After a while Jock suddenly had an idea, and said to Mr Frater 'come on, lets go down to Spittal'! The car already contained a supply of beer, so they set off for Spittal where they spent the day enjoying themselves on the beach.

However, the Frater household in Dingleton became anxious when the husband failed to return from what was normally a short Sunday morning regular exercise. A search party failed to reveal any sightings and a general alarm was raised.

When Jock and his friend returned very late in the evening, to much distress and annoyance, those acquainted with Hamilton style, soon realised that the expedition had been yet another of his contrived practical jokes.

There was never any malice in Jock's actions, and though both he and his famous Abbey Hotel are both gone, there are still a few of us around, who remember with affection, that particular era in Melrose.

STORIES NEWSTEAD TOLD ME

The stone slab discovered in 1846, during the construction of the railway, had a Boar's head in relief, and bore the badge of the 10th Roman legion.

The buildings with the 15ft high stone walls, at the east end of the village on the railway line, and which we called 'The Auld Station', but later thought to be just a siding, was indeed a station from 1850-1852.

The old thatched cottage at Millmount where Sandy Ross the ploughman lived, was on the Gattonside Haugh at some time, and that before the erection of the Battery Dyke, the course of the Tweed was much closer to Newstead.

On the 15th January 1844, Bill Mack was drowned in the Newstead Well. I haven't yet been told how old Bill was or in which of the many wells, he perished.

On the 16th May 1846 the railway at Newstead had just begun.

John Smith the Darnick builder, completed his work on the 'Anna' Battery in August 1827, thus confining and deflecting the course of the Tweed towards Newstead. Today it is known as the Battery Dyke.

When staying at Floors Castle with the Duke of Roxburghe in 1867, Queen Victoria on route to see Melrose Abbey, "came past an immense railway viaduct. The little village, or rather town of Newstead, which we passed through is very narrow and steep", quoted from the book "*More Leaves from the Journal of a Life in the Highlands*"

William Bell a builder came to Newstead from Dryburgh in disgrace. He was obliged to leave Dryburgh by the 11th Earl of Buchan and others, disgusted at his destruction of the Abbey, "pulling down more stones of Dryburgh Abbey than any man before him". He died in Newstead in 1734 but his bones were however brought back to Dryburgh.

Sir Arthur Conan Doyle in his *"Tales of Long Ago"*, includes 'Through the Veil', a short story set in Newstead. It is woven around a Melrose Councillor, one Tom Brown, owner of a grocery store in Melrose High Street, under the title 'Brown and Hanieside', and the experiences when he and his wife drove over to view the excavations at Trimontium.

That the stone buttresses, once visible eighty years ago, then on the south bank of the Tweed above the Boiler or Eddy Pool, at Newstead, and the corresponding paved roadway leading up to Kitty field on the north side, was the site of the Roman bridge which crossed the Tweed.

The large stone at the crest of the hill on the Bogley Burn Road, on the south side, and known to us as the wishing stone, and on which we stood, turning three times to make a silent wish, was the site of the Eildon tree where Thomas the Rhymer met the Queen of the Fairies. Though overgrown, it is still in place today.

Evacuees were lodged in Hazeldean House during the last war.

SONNY HANSON

Herman Gustav Hanson was born in the Mill Cottage Newstead, in 1915. His father, also named Herman, was a German National, who had married a local girl called Jessie Wilson, carried on a hairdressers business in Abbey Street Melrose. They had two sons, the younger called "Sonny", attended Newstead school and was a playmate, although his particular friend was Jimmy Forrest. He was christened by the Reverend Robert James Thompson, Minister of Melrose Parish Church.

During the first World War, Germans in Britain were unpopular and Hanson senior, had a difficult time with anti German feeling running high. To escape attacks, he was often accompanied to Abbey Street, by another Newstead resident, George Ballantyne. Hanson was eventually interned, and considered he had been badly treated by the locals, so he departed for Germany with his family when hostilities ceased. The Hansons of Newstead were soon forgotten.

In October 1939 shortly after the declaration of World War Two, the German Lufftwaffe attacked the Firth of Forth and the railway bridge, this being the first raid on Britain of the war. Spitfires of the Royal Auxiliary Air Force of 603 (City of Edinburgh) and 602 (City of Glasgow) Squadrons shot down two JU88's, being the first enemy aircraft to be destroyed over Britain. One of the badly wounded pilots, asked if he could speak to the Reverend Robbie Thompson, the Minister of Melrose Parish church. Mr Thompson was astonished that the pilot was indeed "Sonny" Hanson, formerly of Newstead. Mr Thompson had actually christened Sonny Hanson in the Mill cottage. Sadly, "Sonny" died of his wounds. His coffin along with others lay in state in St Philip's Church Portobello, guarded by Edinburgh City Police.

By yet another strange coincidence one of the guards was another old Newstead resident, PC Ormiston, who appears on the left of the photograph, taken on 20th October 1939. Afterwards the coffins were accompanied to Edinburgh's Milton Road cemetery, by sixty men of the RAF as thousands of people lined the streets to pay their respects, many coming along out of curiosity, as the cortège passed by. At the graveside a firing party fired a volley over the graves, while pipers of 603 Squadron's band played "Over the Sea to Skye". After the War the bodies were transferred to a German Military cemetery at Cannock Chase.

Lying in State. PC Ormiston is to the left.

TOB LILLICO

On reaching the age of seven at Newstead school, we were transferred to Melrose. We had to walk in all weathers, mostly going by way of Middle Walk which had a well kept cinder path through the great beech trees which lined the sides of the path way. As there were no school meal facilities then, we carried sandwiches, commonly called a 'piece', and tea in tin containers rather similar to small oil cans.

The Melrose gas works, owned by the Curle family, stood at that time, at the school entrance opposite the police station. Old Ned Walker worked the furnaces, stoking and raking out the hot ashes which was eventually sold as coke. The tea tins were handed over to Ned and placed on top of the furnaces to be kept warm. At lunch time we returned to collect them, but the tea was never particularly hot. Coal dust and soot covered everything and although it was an extremely dirty place, at least it was warm. Not a very attractive place to take a meal.

On our return from school to Newstead, we often came by the High Road. The huge billboards on the railway embankment opposite Brown the joiners at East Port, always had fascinating adverts for Bovril, Persil, Castrol motor oil, Cherry Blossom shoe polish and many other products. One was particularly popular depicting a large poster of a Dandy, with monocle, dinner jacket, top hat and cane with the caption "Percy Vere with Oxo". Another advertising quill pens was a rhyme "They came as a boon and a blessing to men, the Pickwick, the owl and the Waverley pen". Often too we would meet the Melrose road sweeper, Tob Lillico. 'Tob' was a nickname, as he was originally from Tobermory in Mull. He was a very tall thin man, with no chin, a small face and mouth surmounted by a large black moustache, very much like Jeff of the then popular American cartoon characters Mutt and Jeff.

Tob when sweeping up leaves, left them in piles on the roadway, often to be kicked about by mischievous school boys. His standard reaction was to threaten us with a "touch of Cherry Blossom" an obvious reference to a kick in the backside.

Unfortunately Tob's active life came about in an accident. His leg was broken when he fell down the outside stairs of the George and Abbotsford Hotel. The Masons walk had just taken place, and the Masons, Tob amongst them, retired to the George and Abbotsford for dinner. The whisky ran out and extra supplies were required. Jock Hamilton the landlord, passed the keys of the wine cellar to the barman with instructions, but a mistake was made and special extra strong 100% proof whisky served in error. This immediately produced disastrous effects, many were overcome by incontinence, incapacity and diarrhoea, others incapable of walking.

Tob Lillico's fall was thought to be related to this, and although he recovered eventually his active life as a sweeper was terminated. However, we all remember Tob with affection, as a friendly, cheerful fellow and one of the great 'characters' of the times.

'Tob' was a larger than life character, and widely known. The photograph shows him posing complete with barrow, horse droppings and broom, in an apparently deserted Melrose Market Square, in the early 1920's. Unusually, considering his occupation, 'Tob' was extremely popular at all levels of Melrose society. The photograph came to me from an unlikely source.

LAWRIE THE GROCER

Thomas Lawrie, was a flourishing Melrose grocer, and his shop was in Abbey street, at the top, with its junction at the Market Square.

He had a large family, most of whom were employed in running the business, which in those days required a considerable labour force, when a delivery service to out laying farms was necessary.

Horse drawn traps delivering orders made extensive journeys to such places as Lilliesleaf, Midlem, Gledswood, Smailholm and many distant villages and farms. Ancrum and Lilliardsedge, a considerable journey from Melrose, was a regular weekly excursion. In return, farms produced eggs from hens, ducks and even turkeys, all for resale in the Abbey street shop.

Lawrie sold large quantities of grapes, which were imported in barrels, packed with granulated cork. The cork, being absorbent was considered as suitable bedding in the stables, but unfortunately turned out to be false economy.

The favourite young horse, known by the name of 'Tammy', one morning was found dead. Its demise from colic was deemed to be due to its having eaten the grape flavoured cork.

This photograph, taken in 1909 shows Lawries' delivery cart near Millmount Farm, Newstead, with Gattonside in the background, and the tree lined Annay Road, as it used to be. Seated in the cart is 'Tucky' Lawrie with the young horse 'Tammy' and John Gordon at its head.

THE LASSES O' MELROSE TOON

by

Piper Jamie Gordon

There's a bonny face in mony a place,
But that's neither up nor doon,
It's a Braw braw lass, that can surpass,
The "Lasses O' Melrose Toon"

They're smart on their feet,
They're aye sae clean and neat,
They're aye sae trig and braw,
At work or oleesure aye the same,
Admired by ane and a'

The auld wives tae, hae seen the day,
When they could haud their ane,
But now you'll mind auld age you'll find,
It never comes it's lane.

There's aye the face, the open grace,
Tho' you search the countrae roond,
You ne'er will find they're else but kind,
The wives O' Melrose Toon.

There's Gala waters braw, braw, Lads,
Ye'll often see them doon,
Aboot the streets, and then they'll meet,
"The Lasses O' Melrose Toon".

HOI POLLOI

BELLA SCOTT

Bella Scott kept the one and only shop at the east end of the village, now Drewen Cottage. It was a general store, selling tobacco and sweets. I remain doubtful however of the hygiene, and only remember making one visit. The sweets bought were mostly liquorice sticks, called locally 'sugar ally', and very hard. Sherbet in triangular paper containers sucked through a hollow liquorice straw was very popular, and cinnamon sticks which could be chewed, or smoked by the more enterprising boys. Liquorice allsorts were an innovation then too.

Bella occupied the bottom part of the house, while her landlord the owner lived upstairs. She also owned and worked a small triangular piece of land, which then formed the junction between the Leaderfoot and Broomhill Roads, known locally as 'Cockit Hat'.

The shop included a Post Office, the Post Box inserted in the wall by the window, looking west, but accessed inside from the shop itself.

JIMMY REDPATH

Known by everyone, though not in his hearing, as 'Jimmy the Po', Jimmy was a bachelor. A tall heavily built man, he spoke slowly in a canny sort of idle fashion, reflecting a general apparently lazy style of life.

He was a joiner by trade, and seems to have spent many years in the restoration of Haggerston Castle. Upon retirement he was given access to a part of the building in St John's Wynd called 'The Old Steading', where upstairs he made writing bureaus for sale. They took many months in the making, so few were produced, but being upstairs they had to be taken out and lowered through a window.

Little boys visiting the workshop frequently resented his unwelcome attentions. The nickname 'Jimmy the Po' was assumed to relate to a time when he lived with his bedridden mother, whose frequent calling for a pottie had been overheard.

WATTIE MORRISON

Wattie was employed as a cook by Captain and Mrs Tulloh at Tannachie. It was unclear just when Wattie came to Newstead, because he was not known to be a native, but he was at Tannachie when I was very young.

Wattie was however a world war one veteran, serving as a cook in the pioneer corps. He used to recount how he came to be, as he described it "Hit on bum by a train", and being invalided out of the army. Just how he came to end up with the Tullohs is a mystery.

Mrs Tulloh was a rather pompous lady with delusions of grandeur and a haughty condescending, Lady of the Manor attitude. The Captain, her husband, also considered himself superior, and ruled the Boy's Club with, at times, bad tempered discipline.

Wattie was viewed as a chef, but this would have been an exaggerated description, so he and Mrs Tulloh were constantly at war.

Particular problems arose when the Tulloh's entertained the Minister of the English Church, or some other local dignitary and Wattie's problems in serving the port at the proper room temperature. Wattie was frequently threatening to leave when his work was challenged, but somehow the uneasy relationship endured.

Wattie lived in at Tannachie, so the accommodation may have been a consideration. On retirement he moved to a disused agricultural labourer's house in St John's Wynd. During his employment little was seen of him in the village, but gossip from the daily help circulated, especially regarding the many domestic disputes in Tannachie House.

Wattie, a bachelor had an effeminate disposition, and unkindly described as a 'Jessie' by the locals.

JOHNNY DOUGLAS

Johnny Douglas was the groom and coachman employed by Captain Tulloh at Tannachie. He lived with his wife and five children in Tannachie Cottage. The old retaining wall continued from the west end of the village up to Tannachie gate, and was not broken as it is today, so the access to the cottage was via narrow stone steps with an iron handrail. Johnny being a horsey man was a keen gambler, and daily could be seen on his journeys, sneaking away from his work, up to the post office to place his shilling bet on some horse that had taken his fancy. He was always bemoaning either his bad luck or bad jockeys, for he seldom admitted to winning. As everyone in the village had a nickname in those days, he was known to the boys, for some obscure reason, as Johnny Butterbum.

Grooms and horse handlers when brushing down horses had a curious habit of hissing through their teeth, very obvious then with so many horses in use, but unfamiliar to many today. So when the Tannachie pony was replaced by an old bull nosed Morris Cowley motor car, old habits seemed to die hard. Willie Cleaver recalls that when Johnny was washing the car, timidly asking why he was hissing through his teeth, the reply was "to keep the stoor from the horses back from getting into my nostrils".

It seemed sensible not to enquire further, so perhaps the acquaintance with horses and car horsepower were at times confusing to old Johnny.

In the confines of a narrow village community at that time, such actions, utterances and inconstancies were more open to observation than they are today, but it did at least add a certain charm to the everyday proceedings and amusement.

We still fondly remember wee Johnny Douglas.

THE BOY IN THE TRAIN

As a very small boy, travelling with my parents by train from Melrose to Edinburgh, and passing Heriot Station, observing some shaggy Highland cattle, I excitedly called out "Oh, look at the Kylies!". (Highland cattle are of course called Kyloes.)

Passengers generally sat incommunicado so I suddenly felt embarrassed, even at that young age. However, much later, the following poem "The boy in the train" has a certain sympathetic significance. Kirkcaldy, it should be pointed out was the linoleum manufacturing centre in Scotland.

THE BOY IN THE TRAIN

Whit way does the engines say 'toot toot'
Is it feart to gang in the tunnel?
Whit way is the furnace no pit oot
When the rain gangs doon the funnel?

❖　　❖　　❖

What will I hae for my tea the night?
A herrin or maybe a haddie.
Has Granma gotten electric light?
Is the next stop Kirkcaldy?

❖　　❖　　❖

There is a hoodie craw on yon turnip raw
And seagulls, sax or seevin.
I'll no fa' oot o' the window Ma
It's sneckit, as sure as I'm leevin.

❖　　❖　　❖

We are in the tunnel, we are all in the dark
But dinna be frichtit Daddy,
We will soon be coming to Beveridge Park
And the next stops Kirkcaldy.

Is yon the moon I see in the sky?
It is awfully wee and curly.
See! there is a coo and a calf ootbye
And a lassie puin a hurley.

He has chackit the tickets and given them back,
So gie me my ain yin Daddy.
Lift doon the bag frae the luggage rack
For the next stops Kirkcaldy.

There is a gie wheen boats at the harbour mouth
And oh! do you see the cruisers?
The cinnamon drop, I was sookin the noo
Has tummelt and stuck in my troosers.

I'll soon be ringing my Granma's bell
She will cry "come in my laddie"
For I ken mysel by the queer like smell
That the next stops Kirkcaldy.

CIRCUSES AND SHOWS

Such simple entertainments that were available in my younger days, were highlighted to a great extent by annual appearances of the then ever popular Circuses and Shows. Visits by Sangers, Bertram Mill's and Pinder's circuses were the life blood, appealing to the natural attraction to animals of the largely rural community, and a general interest in wild beasts.

Certainly it was the case in my family, where at an early age we were always in attendance when a circus appeared. The 'Shows' as they were commonly called were of course the equivalent of the American Carousel and the Italian Jostrie.

The circuses were located in Galashiels, in the public park bordering the road to Selkirk, and the erection of the big top tent was a source of great interest and wonderment at the expertise required in the process.

Sanger's Circus was the most regular of the visitors and in later years acquired or assumed, the title of Lord John Sanger's Circus. Lion tamers, bareback riders, red Indians, trapeze artists and performing elephants, were the principal features, assisted by clowns. Music was provided by a small band of instrumentalists. Spectators sat on wooden benches quite close to the ringside so occasionally, often on purpose water from clownish antics was unavoidable, thus adding to the general amusement.

Attitudes and opinions vary today regarding the circus, but certainly the younger generation is deprived of the opportunity and experiences of an ancient form of entertainment.

The Shows again mostly appearing in Galashiels, but sometimes Melrose, were something completely different, being an association of roundabouts, swings, boxing booths, freak shows, shooting stalls, coconut shies, hoopla stalls and many other games of chance.

Strongmen tested themselves by striking with a large wooden hammer a pin which projected a marker upwards on a metal scale. A bell at the top, if struck resulted in a prize, but this was not often achieved. The coconut shies meant a triangular target of three nuts apparently easy to hit, but not so easy to dislodge with the light weight wooden balls provided. Payment was required before any attempts. The shooting stalls provided air guns firing darts. The targets being light celluloid ping-pong balls rising and falling on a jet of water. Hoopla stalls provided wooden rings at a price, with the opportunity to lasso a variety of articles such as cut glass vases, watches etc., which became yours if successful. The rings however were seldom large enough for the purpose. Prizes were hard to come by as the basic idea was to part people from their money, but a gold fish in a bowl, a coloured balloon or the odd coconut seemed to provide adequate satisfaction to lucky winners.

Boxing booths were always a great attraction to young men, but often hazardous as the professional boxer in the ring issued a challenge to anyone in the audience to fight him for £5 or so. If there was no response, which was often, the case, he would throw a pair of boxing gloves at a particular individual, who to save face often was forced into the ring.

The freak shows were often more embarrassing than entertaining, comprising dwarfs, fat ladies, tattooed men, albinos or deformed or miniature animals. The tent, being separate was not attractive to every taste, and poorly patronised, so the viewer was often alone. To gaze at such unfortunates, and to meet their eyes, was to me at least, a disturbing experience.

The show people and stall owners lived in caravans on the site, and all in some style. The caravans were particularly well appointed and smartly painted, with much chrome used on the exterior finishing. They were mostly drawn by horses, ponies or steam engines.

Time has however moved on, and all the endless noise of music from numerous stalls, plus screaming girls, and the endless chugging of the steam engines, whose connecting belt drove the machinery and provided the lights, can just still be recalled from memories of those happy days long gone.

A DREAM

by

Piper Jamie Gordon

The scene it was a market square,
No far frae Melrose Station,
and sic a crood had gathered there,
Tae haud some celebration.

❖   ❖   ❖

The square was packed tae overflow,
They jostled yin another,
for sic a flock o' famous folk,
Hed ne'er been seen the gither.

❖   ❖   ❖

The air was rent wi' shouts and cheers,
that followed in succession,
then at a word, with one accord,
They formed in procession.

❖   ❖   ❖

Provost Mark, he led the way,
The scene was maist entrancin,
Wi' Jonnie Brough and Jimmy Cheuch,
On steeds o' mettle prancin.

❖   ❖   ❖

Tin Jimmie, he was next tae come,
Wi' blunderbus and sabre,
Then Dank and Tob and Dandy Rob,
And Tony Jock and Taber.

Black Davie came in native dress,
Wi' Willie Rae the plooman,
Then Fat San Toy and Sandy Roy,
And auld Jock Dodds the cooman.

Tammie Boston and his dog,
Wi' Ingram the teacher,
Big Tam Glen and Phil McLean,
And Ritchie Hill the Preacher.

Wull Rudd o' Darnick he cam next,
Wi' Dewar the shoe-maker,
Then Eckie Boo cam pushin' through,
Wi' Tory Knox the baker.

Whitemi Jock came in his cairt,
Weel whitwashed tae the middle,
And following him was Jimmie Sim,
Tam Hart and Johnnie Riddle.

Bob Mercer next cam into view,
Wi' hefty big Tam Blackie,
And Creamie, wi' his Oxford Blue,
Was partneered by the Jaikie.

Then R S Dewar came along,
Disguised as the protector,
And Davie Melrose airm in airm,
Wi' Scougall the Inspector.

Granny Boyd in full war kit,
His bayonet aye kept fixin',
Beside him marched the famous twins,
Robbie and Archie Dickson.

Auld Tidy Mercer he cam next,
Decked up just like a Frenchman,
Then came the famous Light Brigade,
The Gonger and his Henchmen.

O' armour they had nane ava'
They had neither shot no'r poother,
But on each hip a bottle o' thrip,
And a leather ower their shooter.

Drucken Roxburgh he cam next,
In full dress of a sailor,
Wi' Robbie Sheil and Big Daw Neill,
And Snuffy Jeemes the Tailor.

And Mabon wi' his auld dun coo,
cam on wi' Wullie Brockie,
Rob Hutchison frae Darnick View,
Alang wi' Stiltie lockie.

Then Geordie Manface he cam next,
Along wi' Baggy Slater,
Toosh Cook and Tick and Wullie Dick,
Dod Bunyan and Tam Frater.

Jockie Blecknin and his creel,
And Shore cam wi' his bugle,
Robbie Deas and Johnnie Lees,
Wull Bell and Spankie Scougall.

Then Archie Blake the Theeker cam,
Alang wi' Robbie Fowler,
Jock o' the Forge and Honest George,
Wi' his Aide de Camp, the Growler.

Jimmie the Snob and Tilly Bob,
And Geordie Storrie frae the quarry,
Auld Robbie Bird and Tam the Herd,
Dod Grant and Andrae Lawrie.

The Andersons and Sandersons,
The Hendersons and Townies,
Pop Ticket was in rear command,
On yin o' Fishies Pownies.

Hark! what was that-a bugle note,
that through the air comes drivin',
And in East Port the guns they snort,
Prince Robert is arrivin'.

He passed the Ship without a nip,
This made a great impression,
And in his unassuming way,
He joined the grand procession.

They then marched three times round the cross,
Wi' flags and banners fleein'
And by my faith as shair as daith,
It was a sight worth seein'.

Doon tae the Cudd's Green they gang,
Tae haud a jubilation,
Where Granny Curle's wa' is hung,
Wi' flags o' every nation.

The Brewry cairts are roond the bend,
Weel packed wi' beer and rations,
A platform is at the end,
On which appears Galashans.

The Dank recited Rhoderick Dhu,
And man was made to mourn,
Bob Mercer sang Flat Fitted Jean,
And I'm a Scotsman born.

Manface, he gave feats o' strength,
And Creamie played the fiddle,
Wull Rudd, he danced the Heilan Fling,
Alang wi' Johnie Roddell.

Tin Jimmie sang the Anchors Weighed,
It wad hae made a cat sick,
Black Davie played the mandoline,
While Taber did the hat trick.

Johnnie Lee then gave a song,
But nane could understand him,
And Davie Melrose looped the loop,
On auld Camlachie's Tandem.

Then auld San Toi and Sandy Roy,
Theyr tried to sing a duet,
But big Dod Bunyan he got up,
And pelted them wi' suet.

Tob sang the Wolf and Memories Dear,
And Mbon sang the Diver,
Then Stiltie Lockie said he'd dance
The Gonger for a fiver.

The Gonger he took up the bet,
And said he'd make it doyuble,
Then Eckie Boo stole Mason's coo,
And this caused all the trouble.

This was the signal for a fecht,
They tackled yin another,
And in the fray 'tis sad to say,
The Gonger lost his leather.

They focht like demons in a cage,
Sic roarin' and sic screamin',
Five on the clock when I awoke,
And found I had been dreamin.

FUR AND FEATHER

The Newstead flour mill activities terminated about 1924. The mill itself, and the Mill House were occupied afterwards by a Mrs Geddes and her son Norman. They had decided to convert it into a fur farm, an unusual venture at that time. Bob Mills an acknowledged animal expert from Denny in Stirlingshire and Sidney Jacobson from Lowestoft were engaged as managers, and later another, whose name escapes me came down from Buckie in Banffshire.

All the many floors of the old Mill were converted for the breeding of rabbits in large numbers, all of a single breed, known as Chinchilla. The live rabbits were exported to the Continent, and the numbers produced in the Mill itself were augmented by stocks from the villagers. The boys in the village were presented with a doe, in kindle, viz. pregnant, and the resulting litters of young rabbits were bought back by the firm. I was one of the boys who participated in this scheme, which was great fun.

In addition to rabbits, large pens were erected on each side of the Middle Walk to Melrose. On the south side were Blue and Silver foxes, while on the north and towards the Mill stream were Muskrats, Coypu and a large South American fur bearing animal called Viscaccia, as well as fitch, a type of mink.

The Muskrats eventually escaped into the dam, but even today, seventy two years later, the cement artificial muskrat pond can still be seen from the Middle Walk. None of those animals were bred successfully, no doubt due to unsuitable conditions, and lack of management expertise. The demand for live rabbits also declined, and the Geddes family then took to breeding dogs. Borzois and Pekinese. The Borzois being tall and athletic were always a cause for anxiety when confronted and usually best to be avoided whenever possible. The fur farm venture however eventually declined, and the Geddes' departed.

The next occupant converted the premises into a mushroom growing business, with limited success for a few years only, the damp conditions necessary for mushrooms hastened the rot of the floors and the final destruction of the Old Newstead Flour Mill.

At that time nearly every villager kept livestock of some sort or another, ranging from pigs, bees, poultry, cage birds, bantams, rabbits, ducks, guinea pigs, fancy mice, pigeons, ferrets and even squirrels. The red squirrels were numerous in the fir woods by the Bogley Burn and the Riddells and Andersons caught and kept them in large cages. The Mitchells at St John's Cottage had hundreds of pigeons. The large house gable being completely occupied by home made wooden Dovecotes. The pigeons were of mixed colours, including White Fantails, and flew to feed on the cornfields in huge flocks.

The Mitchells also had pet Jackdaws taken from the nest holes in the Scaurs above Cowie's Hole by the Tweed. The bees were taken in the autumn to the Heather Moors all with fresh sections for the exclusive Heather Honey. On return the weight of honey in the hive often required three men to carry them from the lorries. Some of the village houses had ceiling hooks for hams to hang during the winter. The pigs of Bill Scott, Briar Cottage and Sid Ovens, Claymires Cottage, were fattened and sold at Newtown market. But the Riddells of Townhead Farm did their own slaughtering and curing. The distressing scene of pigs with their throats cut careering round the farm steading, squealing until they dropped, haunts me even today. Huge vats of boiling water had already been prepared, so that the carcasses could be plotted. This was necessary to remove the hairs by scraping.

Anne Ford, a daughter of Jim Ford of Barnet Head Farm, decided at that time that Angora Rabbit wool, like Cashmere today, would bring her a fortune, so a large hut was put up in the field which is now Rushbank Housing Estate. The rabbits were bred and the wool cut frequently. Newstead was full of entrepreneurs of one sort or another, but alas, so often with a limited view of business principles, many inventive ideas were unsuccessful.

However, in retrospect, I think they were all deserving of credit, and Newstead's ability to produce individuals of vision and perception was a hallmark of those times.

Many households of course kept dogs. Mrs Tulloh, wife of Captain Tulloh of Tannachie had Pekinese, as did Mrs Geddes of the Mill. The two ladies in Hazledean and Peter Nesbit of the Auld Hoose had St Bernards. Cats were scarce. Jack Pringle of Hawthorn Cottage in the Back Road and old Tom Mitchell, from St John's Cottage were well known and active poachers. Both had guns and roamed at will in the fields around the village and on Tweedside. Any cat found roaming outside the village was shot or trapped.

I only remember one cat. Mrs Forrest, who was Jock Pringle's sister lived in Eildon View, on the Main Street. She kept a black cat called Rudy. This cat was her pride and joy, and named after Rudy Valentino, a very handsome and adored popular American film star of the time. Brother Jock, who was very often under the influence of alcohol, an amiable character, with a great sense of humour, on his way home on one occasion he called in to see his sister at Eildon View, sat down on the settee and spotted Rudy. After admiring the cat for a few minutes, he put his hand into his pocket and brought out a ferret, which immediately gave chase to Rudy around the room, knocking down ornaments in the process. The cat was eventually rescued by Mrs Forrest who was not amused, although Jack thought it great fun.

Mrs Tulloh, of Tannachie was a very superior lady, who one day walking in Claymires Lane with her Pekinese, encountered Bell Jardine the Hazledean maid exercising the St Bernard. The Pekinese attacked the St Bernard. Bell who was a simple girl and Mrs Tulloh had angry words, ending with Bell saying "It was your little skitter that started it" unlike today, dogs were cheap to feed. Bones from the butcher and an abundance of rabbits with kitchen scraps made up adequate feeding and veterinary treatment unheard of.

PUBLIC UTILITIES

WATER

As late as 1900, Newstead was without mains water supplies. In March 1901, in a letter to the Melrose District Committee, Curle and Erskine, solicitors to the estate of Lady Fairfax (late of Ravenswood), advised that £500 had been set aside in her Will, for the provision of a water supply for the village of Newstead, and proposing that it be abstracted from the Burgh. It was agreed that the Trustees of Lady Fairfax undertake the construction of the link main with the Burgh. It was further agreed "as only fair and equitable" that a joint Infectious Diseases Hospital be erected within the (to be formed) special water district, the local authorities jointly erecting same, shall pay Lady Fairfax's Trustees a proportion of the capital sum for the main.

The link main was constructed in 1902. Following this decision, seven pump wells, known to us only as pumps, were placed at central positions in the village. One on the Back road, another at the bottom of Barnethead Farm road near Townhead, and a third in St John's Wynd served the east end. The mid village pumps were situated at the east end of the village school, opposite the Fairfax Hall, and at the entrance to the Yiddy, where the village notice board stands today. Another was in Claymires Lane, opposite the Hazeldean House entrance, and the last situated midway between Tannachie Cottage and the Mill on the south side of the main road, opposite Saugh Cottage served the west end villagers.

The pumps were of unusual design and style, and made of cast iron. They stood three feet tall, and were cylindrical in shape, topped by a large domed corrugated head, fixed at the top. They were twelve inches or so in diameter. The turning was a round serrated knob, similar to that seen on pocketwatches, and the interior workings drew water up from deep down, by a chain system as seen on bicycles today. This prevented freezing in winter times.

Prior to this, the village relied on its many open wells and there was never a shortage of water, but of course it required to be transported by hand. There were no indoor supplies and bath water and laundry water had also to be heated on coal fires. Coal fires were a necessity.

Lavatories were invariably located outside the houses and mostly of the dry variety. When the main water supply became available, water closets came into use, but still remained outside. Night time excursions in winter were sometimes eased by the use of chamber pots. The outside closets were kept free of frost by small burning paraffin oil lamps.

Many individual homesteads had their own water pumps which sucked up supplies from deep underground wells, by manipulating an iron handle. These structures were long tall, boxed affairs, which required to be primed with water to induce the suction action to commence.

So, gradually the village water supply evolved, but it would undoubtedly would have been delayed without the initiative, perception and generosity of Lady Fairfax herself.

SOME THINGS YOU DIDN'T KNOW

RAVENS

There were Ravens at Ravenswood in the 1920's, not unfortunately flying wild, but kept in a large aviary enclosed near the North Lodge, backing onto the wall boundary of the A68 road. They actually talked, and being visible to passers by, interested many, especially children.

CORNCRAKES

It was almost impossible to get a proper nights rest, during the summer, when the heat compelled the windows to be kept open. Corncrakes seemingly in every field called incessantly, from dusk to dawn, were cursed by young and old, and impossible to see or be silenced.

PROMISCUITY

At least eight illegitimate children were produced by village maidens during my younger years. Some fathers were known, and the subject attracted keen interest at that time.

THE GENERAL STRIKE

During the General Strike of 1926, Newstead was visited by Newtongrange Miners Pipe Band, who occupied a very large hay barn, which stood at the Newstead entrance to the Middle Walk to Melrose. The barn has long since been removed.

The band stayed for the duration of the Strike, supported by hand-outs and hospitality of the poor villagers. They toured the various towns and villages, performing and collecting donations. The barn and the pipers practising in the evening, was of course, a magnet for the village boys. Some of the female adolescents also found the whole exercise interesting to.

SHOOTING

The Hamiltons of Melrose, owners of the Abbey and George and Abbotsford hotels, owned extensive agricultural property around Newstead as well as Oakendean House.

An abundance of game allowed rough shooting to take place, to be enjoyed by the Hamilton family and friends. On one such expedition, George Hamilton fired through a hedge near Oakendean, carelessly, and shot one of the beaters, old Hogarth, of Melrose. Although peppered with shot, at close range, old Hogarth survived, and recovered.

The affair though discussed frequently by the locals, didn't come to court. An indication of the attitudes prevailing at that time.

HORSE DRAWN CHIP SHOPS

Mobile chip shops, drawn by horses, an unlikely spectacle today, frequently visited the village. One came all the way from Galashiels, and was owned by Adam Hall. The other belonged to Timmy Simpson of Melrose.

The chip shop was a very large, van like vehicle, containing a coal fire with chimney protruding through its roof. The boiling fat was enclosed in a container with a lid cover, to prevent it overflowing when the vehicle was on the move. The raw potatoes were peeled and prepared elsewhere, but chipped on the vehicle by a chipping machine activated by a long handle. There was no water available on the cart, so hygiene was of a doubtful quality.

However, these visits were very popular and business brisk. I do not remember exactly how the horse was driven, or controlled, nor whether there were one or two individuals involved in the trade.

Hall, who came from Galashiels, had to make a considerable journey, so presumably it was a profitable venture. He returned via Leaderfoot and Gattonside on his way home. Pinder's Circus frequently visited the area and renowned for their many colourful horses. Timmy Simpson's horse being a Piebald was therefore known by name of 'Pinder'.

The horse drawn chip shops were unusual, and unfortunately no photographs seem to have survived.

MENAGERIE

In 1922, Bostock and Wombells' menagerie came to Melrose and occupied the entire area of the Market Square with cages of wild animals of all species.

The cages lined the roadway up to the pavements outside the chemist's shop, and the Ormiston Hall, and only one part of the road through was clear, on the north side by the book shop. Numerous spectators, and there were many, fell foul of a nasty leopard, determined to mark his territory, or perhaps in disapproval of his unhappy condition.

After staying two days, they departed, proceeding through Newstead early in the morning, the numerous cages of lions and tigers etc. drawn by horses. The sole elephant however, was somehow left behind, and in racing to catch the others up, the man in charge, and on foot, not being a mahout, accidentally dropped the stick for controlling the elephant, and had no time to gather it up.

Sometime after they had passed, it was recovered by my father, and became a curiosity and an unusual prop for the living room window which didn't possess sash cords, and had to be open in the summer weather.

Strange things happened in the Newstead of old, probably the first and only elephant to traverse the village street.

A SPORTING SPECTACULAR

In May 1931, the annual boys' rugby competition held in Melrose, known as The Crichton Cup, was won for the first and last time, by a team from the village of Newstead. The photograph shows the successful team with the trophy, on a seat taken at the Yiddy.

Back row, left to right:
Pat McQueen, Adam Mitchell, Jim Anderson, Adam Riddell.

Front row, left to right:
Jim Gordon, Joe Martin, Duncan McKinnon.

SOCIAL OCCASIONS AT LEADERFOOT

On most Sunday afternoons during the summer months, the magnet for Newstead village youth was Leaderfoot and the old road bridge. The bridge was built between 1776 and 1780. Leaderfoot comprised the farm occupied by Tom Porteus, and a small community of houses east and west of the main road to Earlston, and Bob Mitchell's Blacksmith shop. One house was distinguished from the others, being of a particular English style of extended wooden adornments in black and white, and an elegant entrance porchway. Although there is no evidence, this perhaps was a Toll House.

None of those houses exist today. As they occupied both sides of the road and formed the corners of a right angled turn from each direction, vehicles approaching were unsighted and there were frequently road accidents. This led to the automobile association posting a permanent official, known as an AA Scout, at the junction, controlling and conducting the traffic. He lodged in Earlston and came daily by motor cycle. This continued until the removal of the houses on the west side.

With so few forms of amusement, the trend in those days, when everyone walked, was for the Earlston people to walk towards Leaderfoot, and the Newstead folks likewise, whilst the Newstead youngsters walked in groups in both directions, chatting, courting girls, and generally all fraternising in the most friendly way. There was no traffic to speak of and the roadways were clear. The big houses of Drygrange, Gledswood and Ravenswood, had large families of retainers and servant girls, all contributing to the social "gaiety whirl" atmosphere of the times.

Leaderfoot Bridge also attracted during the summer, hundreds of nesting House Martins. Every inch of the under parapets on both sides of the bridge was occupied and the flow to and fro, of the breeding birds was an unforgettable spectacle for a naturalist. Sadly there are none today.

Some of the older boys of less social or amorous tendencies, congregated at an area, at the south end of the bridge, where they played a game called "pitch and toss", unknown to many today. This was played by each one pitching a penny up to a marker, rather similar to quoits. The nearest to the marker then collected all the coins into the palm of his hand, tossing them into the air, and every penny that landed heads up, became his for the keeping. Whatever remained was similarly treated by the next nearest to the marker until all the pennies had gone. Then they started again. As this was a type of gambling and illegal, the police frequently disrupted activities.

Today such simple uncomplicated activities seem insignificant, but the attitude eighty years ago had a certain rustic style, entertaining but less frenetic than it is today.

THE RAILWAY PEOPLE

Newstead's railway associations most likely stem from the village's close proximity to the constructors original line of the London and North Eastern Railway from London to Edinburgh, and the building of the Leaderfoot railway viaduct for the Berwickshire railway.

It is known that the many Irish labourers engaged in its construction lodged in the village at that time. Many alas succumbed to an epidemic of cholera which swept the country at that period. Those unfortunates now rest in Melrose Abbey churchyard. This area in the south west corner at the junction of Abbey Street, and the middle walk appears to be unoccupied, and has no marked headstones.

It is thought that there were at least three lodging houses in Newstead at that time. One on the east side of the Mill House, standing in the area now occupied by Still's garden. The second and main house, always referred to as the Lodging House, was of two stories, and stood in the area now containing the four new houses in the Main Street, between the Auld Hoose and Briar Cottage. A wooden gate at the west end, allowed access to a substantial garden on the south between the building and the burn. On the east, it was bounded by a stone depot where stones, for the metalled road were kept.

In the nineteen twenties, at least nine Newstead families were engaged in railway work, and in a variety of duties. Three were signalmen, one a booking office clerk, one the ganger Bob Turnbull, who lived in Railway Cottage, and four were surfacemen. Jock Cowie was an electrician. Bill Tait who lived in Rikkieburn, was the signalman at Ravenswood Junction. Willie Henderson the booking clerk lived in Claymires Lane, whilst Davie Forrest a signalman at Melrose was in Eildon View.

The surfacemen were employed on track maintenance also scything the long grass which grew on the railway banks during the summer months and which was made into hay. At intervals, on the line, were wooden huts, as shelters for the men and tools and where meals were taken, they also acted as shelters from the weather. There was always considerable freight and passenger traffic, and all punctual to the minute.

Whole trainloads of Americans arrived to visit the Scott Country, staying three days in the various hotels in Melrose. On Melrose Rugby Sports Day, hundreds arrived by special trains from Hawick, Gala and Edinburgh. The younger members of the Royal family were frequent guests of the Duke of Buccleuch at Eildon Hall, and joined the late Pullman from Edinburgh to London at Melrose.

The LNER engines all had names, such as "SIR WALTER SCOTT", "THE UNION OF THE SOUTH AFRICA", "MARMION", " WAVERLEY" and many others. The signal box at Ravenswood controlled the junction where the line divided to Earlston and Berwickshire.

Mrs Mitchell and her daughter Annie of Burnfoot Cottage, Newstead.

The track on the viaduct was two feet or so below the pedestrian platform, thus allowing a train to overtake workmen and pass in safety. It was forbidden to non-railway pedestrians.

The viaduct's history contains at least one notable suicide, which I remember attracted considerable interest at the time. On 13th April 1928, Charles Sims, an artist and member of the Royal Academy, leapt from the railway viaduct and fell 150 feet into the swirling waters of the Tweed. Sims was commissioned to make a portrait of the King, but it was withdrawn from the Royal Academy exhibition when His Majesty disapproved. Sims was deeply depressed, and suffered from insomnia, but came to Ravenswood as a guest of Mr Younger.

THE KIRK

To my knowledge, between the wars, Newstead folk although no doubt religiously inclined, were not avid church attenders. Various reasons present themselves.

Life was hard, people worked long hours and shops remained open late, so many tired workers, whose free time only was on the Sabbath Day, probably felt it should truly be a day of rest. No doubt, personal, household, or domestic chores, garden work, or caring for livestock also was time consuming in what was for many a harsh existence. Church then, took second place.

However, children were made to attend Sunday school, and religious instruction part of the normal day school teaching. As tiny tots we attended church teachings in the Fairfax Hall, where the Deaconesses reigned. Then, at an older age, we walked each Sunday from Newstead to Melrose to attend Sunday school at Melrose Parish church.

At that period we were blessed by having a truly remarkable and much loved Minister of the Parish church, in the Reverend R J (Robbie) Thompson. An Aberdonian, Robbie Thompson involved himself in nearly every aspect of local community affairs, and was an enthusiastic historian, and active supporter of the Trimontium Roman excavations.

His church magazine notes were not entirely given over to religious affairs, but often included items of historical interest, well researched and obviously with a view to conservation. He was immensely popular, particularly in Newstead, where he would suddenly arrive, without prior warning to partake of afternoon tea, or meals going at the time. He loved chatting on many topics, village gossip and such goings on, but seldom religion.

There was a general feeling that his great opportunities for compensation against the unenthusiastic church members, came at Communion Services at the Parish church. By preaching exceptionally lengthy services, often extending well after one o' clock, worshippers were compelled to walk back to Newstead, unhappy at being so late for the midday meal. Communion then was looked upon with apprehensive dread. However, all was soon forgiven and Robbie became once again as friendly and popular as ever.

His Christenings were performed in the homes, when great efforts were made to provide suitable meals afterwards. Weddings also were frequently conducted at home, and funeral services likewise, prior to the customary final service in internment at the cemetery.

At the time of my Christening in February 1916, at Fortune Row, Newstead, I was presented with a Holy Bible, suitable inscribed by Mr Thompson. This was an exceptional and unusual gesture then, and it was not repeated for my brother four years later, nor in the case of any other known villager born at that time. He was also the guardian of many local historical treasures in Newstead and Melrose.

When a proposal to widen the Middle Walk from Melrose to Newstead at the Abbey Street entrance, was raised, he revived the spectre of cholera, if the remains of the Irish cholera victims lying in that area were to be disturbed. In Newstead he was enthusiastic about retaining the old "loupin' on stanes", in the village, particularly he urged my mother to inform him if the special stone at the St John's Lane entrance was ever removed. Alas today it has gone. There can be few, if any, Ministers of Robbie Thompson's calibre in the church today, given that churches and attitudes have also changed, but Robbie, with his Jesuit style black hat and cloak is unforgettable.

VISITATION FROM OUTER SPACE

Newstead's ability to produce surprises, is it seems unending, and the following account of a meteorite descending upon the village is a revelation even today, to the few survivors of that particular era.

A meteorite was discovered in 1827 by a Mrs Kate Williamson while digging out a sunken cellar for a new cottage. Some doubt exists as to the exact location of the find, but old records describe the site as being on "the south side of the road near the east end of the village, and a group of three cottages at right angles beyond which a narrow cross road turns southward into the valley behind, past one of the village wells, and crosses a little streamlet".

Mrs Williamson was digging out pits for coals etc., when at a depth of four feet she found the large piece of what appeared to be native iron.

George Burnet, a mason to trade, who lived a few doors down the village, took it home. He died in 1842, and his brother Frances Burnet, who became the Right Worshipful Master of the Masonic Lodge, in 1845, then moved into his late brother's house. He built a

stone wall around the garden, and put in it an old stone trough, on its side. Here the iron meteorite lay for thirty five years.

The Burnets were known to have occupied the Auld Hoose, and an old stone trough is in the east wall of the Auld Hoose at the present time. It has long been a source of curious discussion, unusual as it is.

John Smith, a local gentleman, was convinced it was "Native Iron" and meteoric, and took it to Edinburgh where it was tested by Dr. Murray Thomson, a lecturer on chemistry.

It was then passed to Mr Young, a lapidary and cut into two portions. The meteorite weighed 32lb 11oz, and was 10¾ inches long. It was a dark reddish brown colour, almost black in some parts, with spots of brighter red in places. The two portions were described as solid, dense and steel like in appearance throughout, and the colour beautifully white bright, like steel.

Plaster casts of the original were made by a Mr Alex Stewart, who offered them for sale at a very moderate price, to anyone wishing to possess a facsimile of a rare Scottish meteoric iron. It is believed to have been the largest meteorite that has been discovered in Britain to date.

The Newstead meteorite now reposes in the National Museum in Chambers Street, Edinburgh.

FAIRFAX COTTAGE

Christine Clark, one of Willie Clark's daughters, married Malcolm Cleaver, a highland lad who came to Newstead to assist Dr James Curle's excavations at Trimontium. They were married in the top floor of the Auld Hoose opposite the War Memorial. The house was divided then and the entrance to the top part was by way of an outside stone stairway with iron hand railings which protruded into the main roadway. The bottom part was entered by the lane, and occupied by a farm servant employed at Town Head.

The Cleavers were married in the bow windowed room, but moved to No. 1 Fortune Row where their three children were born. When the Fairfax Hall was opened, the family moved as caretakers into Fairfax Cottage, a two storey house at the gates to the Hall, where the present War Memorial rests. The accommodation was rent free. By this time the Trimontium excavations had been completed, but Malcolm Cleaver was retained as an employee of Dr Curle, and was his gardener at Priorswood for twelve years, until his death.

Unfortunately he lost his right hand and arm in a threshing machine accident, at Curle's farm at Millmount. The Cleaver family kept the Fairfax Hall and its grounds in an immaculate condition, and I have referred to this admiration in my notes on Fairfax.

The Cleavers were married in June 1911, and on the day of her wedding, Christine Clark was scrubbing down the old stone stairway, which I have described elsewhere, which lead onto the road at that time.

Old Adam Riddell, from the farm was passing, and said she had brought bad luck on herself, and would be condemned to work hard for the rest of her life.

She often reflected on this, and how true the superstition proved to be.

THE EAST END

This photographic scene depicts a flavour of village life many years ago. The date is uncertain but thought to be late eighteenth century. The buildings on the left were removed about 1901. This occurred when Lady Harriet Fairfax bequeathed to the village, in memory of her late husband Admiral Sir Henry Fairfax, a mission hall, library and a Deaconess' house.

Admiral Fairfax lived at Ravenswood and the buildings stood on land he owned. The Deaconess' house remains on the site, but it is now privately owned.

The photograph shows a horse and carriage stationary outside 'Mud Mile' pub. The sign above the door has just been taken down.

'Mud' Miles surprisingly was a female, and 'Mud' may have been an affectionate term for mother.

What is known however is that lacking public conveniences, male clients were wont to relieve themselves against a gable wall of Tweedview, shown on the left. Tweedview was obviously built before Lady Fairfax's activities. There has been speculation regarding the coach and the gentleman with the coachman.

Three big houses to the east of Newstead were at that time the residences of Mr Roberts (Drygrange), Lord George Scott MP (Gledswood) and the Fairfax family (Ravenswood).

It is possible that Mr Roberts sits in the carriage. The Post Office sign is visible on the gable of Briar Cottage, occupied in my youth by Bill Scott who was employed as a railway surfaceman. The Post Office later became part of Bella Scott's (no relation) general shop, shown at top right with the sign just visible above the door.

The cart in the top background bears the lettering "Gray and Sons, Aerated Waters, Galashiels", and was possibly making a delivery to Bella Scott.

The open area on the right with the bollards contained what was known then as a stone depot, holding road mending materials. It was positioned to supply coarse stones on the steepest part of the hill in winter, when roads were difficult, it was still in use when I was young.

Many of the big draft horses drawing trees through the village to the Earlston sawmill used to fall at this part of the hill, with often much damage to their knees.

The remnants of the old Lodging House are just visible at the bottom right of the picture. It was reputed to have housed many of the Irish labour force during the construction of the railway. Traces of the old foot causeway shown on the left are still visible today, although mostly covered by the tar surface. Some of Newstead's famous sundials can clearly be seen.

NEWSTEAD SECRETS

It is surprising that when the Melrose Festival pilgrimage annually descends upon Newstead to pay homage at the ruins of the first Masonic lodge, so little of its vast history is promulgated to the enthusiastic followers, young and old.

William Heatley, a noted artist who lived at No 1 St John's Cottage, was commissioned to make a sketch in 1891, when a fiat was issued that it should be demolished. According to records, it had stood for 280 years. Heatley reveals it as a substantial two story building, surrounded by a low wall and fencing with a lean-to on the east gable.

The window over the door was very finely carved with the inscription "al Glorie be to God, Com Lord Isves if God Ivstifie Vho Vil Condem".

At the time of demolition this window was taken by the Masons of Melrose for their lodge. The only other find was an antique ink bottle and an old rusty pair of compasses, which were acquired by Mr William Hart of Burnside Cottage, Newstead.

The house was built in 1613 by Robert Mein, and masonic meetings held there until 1743.

A vast amount of interesting material is on record, and one would have thought some extracts (in leaflet form) if produced at the festival ceremony, would add lustre and variety to the proceedings.

Dare we suggest this idea to the organisers?

NEWSTEAD BEFORE DESTRUCTION

This photograph taken in 1930 shows a group of girls, at what was known as Beatties Corner, and the junction road leading to the Yiddy. The lovely old trees, and the ancient walls along with the houses in the background, have sadly now gone.

Their demolition by a developer, whose further plans were refused, has resulted in a legacy of an unsightly area of jagged unfinished walls, and a green area of doubtful recreational value to the village.

The red standing stone in the field behind, but masked by the trees, was the pedestrian crossing of the burn, when originally it ran across the top of the road. The burn is now piped underneath leading to its joining with the Mill Dam. The standing stone is unmarked but bears a small lead insert with the initials FRNC 1895. This relates to Fred Curle, a Melrose lawyer, and brother of Dr James Curle, of Trimontium fame, whose family owned extensive land in Newstead, and the field where the stone now rests.

The girls have just come from rehearsals at Captain Tulloh of Tannachie's Club, for a showing of HMS Pinafore, which explains the unusual dress wear.

The house in the background of the photograph was the scene of an unusual accident in 1939. Jim Lothian who lived in the village of Redpath, had a greengrocers business of sorts, growing vegetables and selling tomatoes, lettuce, cabbages etc. from a horse drawn flat cart to the Newstead villagers. At that time, the 6th Battalion of the Kings Own Scottish Borderers has been assembled preparing for war and on a route march. Advancing from Leaderfoot and on approaching the Newstead hospital, the Pipe Band was given the order to play. The loud initial beating of the big drum startled Jim Lothian's horse, which at that time was at the top east end of the village. The horse then careered off with cart attached, down the steep hill to the corner, which it failed to negotiate, crashing finally into the doorway and killing itself in the process. Runaway horses were not uncommon, but few resulted in tragedy.

Left to right:
Ruby Cowie, Ina Douglas, Netta Purdom, Ella Gill, Mamie Cowie,
Mary Davidson, Annie Mitchell and Jenny Gill.

Front:
Isa Mitchell.

THE YARROW "THRONE"

In 1899, a Melrose cabinet-maker, McDonald of Buccleuch Street, Melrose, made a rather special chair. Crafted from a variety of woods, mainly Walnut, Mahogany, Ebony, Cherry and with Satinwood inlay, the chair was commissioned by Sir William Strang-Steel of Philiphaugh, Selkirk. It bears the sign McDonald on the underside of the seat, and the date 1899 is on the back. It is thought that it was commissioned for the Paris exhibition of 1899, but it now resides in an obscure Hall in Yarrow Selkirkshire.

Its re-discovery fell to Jim Blake the hall caretaker, who on cleaning it one day was surprised to find the name McDonald Melrose on the underside of the seat. His curiosity aroused he set off on the twenty mile journey to Melrose, where enquiries led him to me at Newstead. As a cabinet-maker I worked for Johnstone and Aitchison who took over the business in Melrose from McDonald when his business was destroyed by fire. My superiors had been McDonald employees, and craftsmen of a high order, and of course the name McDonald was known to me, so it was exciting.

Made in the style of a large Coronation type throne, the chair has carved unicorns supporting the arms and a beautiful centre marquetry panel depicting a Rampant Lion and St Andrew's cross with a crown over the Rampant Lion Shield. At each corner of the back panel are four Elizabethan crowns, various shields, each of a different Coat of Arms, surround the back of the chair. The domed top piece depicts St Andrew, leading four disciples, and overhead the motto, NEMO ME IMPUNE LACESSET. The panels supporting the arms of the chair show elaborate Prince of Wales' feathers and surrounded by HONI SOIT QUI MAL Y PENSE. As long as anyone can remember the chair has been in Yarrow Hall. It is in perfect condition, even the horns of the unicorns, which you would have expected to have been damaged or broken after all this time, are unmarked.

This Yarrow Hall in Selkirkshire was a gift to the people of the valley from the then Sir William Strang-Steel, but the present

Sir William can not shed any light on the chair, and knows nothing of any family connection. The chair's history has yet to be uncovered, but it is indeed a gem, and something quite special, deserving a better repose than to remain under dust sheets in an obscure community hall in the Yarrow Valley.

The photograph shows the magnificent throne, and on the left Jim Blake the Hall Caretaker and on the right Jim Gordon, sometime cabinet-maker of Melrose.

ALAN COBHAM'S FLYING CIRCUS

In the summer of 1933, Newstead had an unusual and exciting visitation in the form of Alan Cobham's Flying Circus. Sir Alan was a famous English aviator born in 1894, who had served in World War One with the Royal Flying Corps. On cessation of hostilities he reverted to civil aviation. He took part in many long distance flights, and pioneered the London to Cape Town route. In 1926 he was awarded the Britannia Trophy for a flight to Australia and back.

It was also he who devised the system for refuelling planes in the air, so was quite famous at the time he came to Newstead with his aeroplanes. They were still a novelty then, and it was a great surprise when he arrived with his aircraft at the Trimontium Roman Camp site. This of course was a business venture.

The planes were light, two seaters, with one propeller, and fifteen minutes sightseeing flights over Melrose and around the Eildon hills cost five shillings. This was a considerable sum in those days of very low wages, so very few villagers had the opportunity to take advantage of the perceived glamour of actually flying.

Many of the brave enthusiasts were naturally unacquainted with the technicalities of flight and anxious customers were heard as the 'plane trundled uneasily over the uneven field on take off, calling out, "what about the belts?", obviously expecting to be strapped in. Others had trouble with head gear, as hats could be seen fluttering down from the heights over the village, all adding to the novelty and amusement of the occasion.

When the circus had gone, they left behind many large petrol drums at Trimontium, providing a boon for Willie Anderson, who spent many days thriftily draining the remains to fuel his old motor bike.

Such abandoned litter then, seems to have been a precursor of what is so familiar to us all today.

THE BAND OF HOPE

The common alcohol addictions of many men in those early days, and the almost daily spectacle of drunken individuals on the street, naturally induced much concern, and a strong temperance movement became established. The Hotel at Palma Place, Melrose, now the Country Kitchen cheese shop, was the Temperance Hotel. Burt's Hotel also was temperance, at that time.

Many people were active in the temperance movement, targeting the youth, especially boys, and the Church hall, at Church Place, Melrose was the regular meeting place. Miss Betty Allan of the congregational Church, Melrose was a leading activist, ably assisted by Mr John Hart and many others.

Almost all the local Melrose and Newstead boys were members, attracted no doubt by the cinematography films and slides of African natives and wild life. I particularly remember those produced by Martin Johnston an American explorer. Very much "Saunders of the River". Tea and cookies followed before we had to repeat our pledge against alcohol:

> I promise here by grace divine
> To touch no spirits, ale or wine
> Nor will I serve to others while I live, strong drink
> In this my pledge no drink to take
> And also for my neighbour's sake
> No drink, no drink, no drink for me.

At the end of each meeting a collection was taken, and during this proceeding we sang a ditty. I can only recall two lines:

> Hear the pennies dropping
> Hear them one by one etc...

Nicknames for every one and every thing was a feature of the times, and so 'The Band of Hope' became known to us boys, as the 'Band of Toots'. I also must confess that I have broken my pledges since then!

THE NEWSTEAD PICNIC

Shortly after the First world war, and when village life gradually returned to normal, the village elders decided to arrange an outing for the entertainment of all residents and all ages, but particularly for the children.

This became an annual event and because it was held in the summer, became to be known by everyone as, "The Newstead Picnic". A suitable day and venue was decided on and, assembled villagers conveyed in open topped motor charabancs hired for the occasion.

The very first such picnic was held no further afield than Drygrange, in the grounds of the Big House. All I can recall of that outing, was that foot races and high jumping for children of various ages were arranged. We were each given a paper bag of various buns to eat with tea. There must have been some sort of football too, as a ball kicked very high descended unexpectedly, on my dear mother's head, and knocked her to the ground, causing much distress at the time.

Over the years, the organisers became more adventurous, or perhaps their accumulation of funds improved, for visits were made to Newton Don at Kelso, Floors Castle, Spittal (many times) Portobello, and the last for me, and the most enjoyable was North Berwick, when we sailed round the Bass Rock, on a gloriously hot day.

The Newstead Picnics have long been discontinued, and another aspect of community life in those times, gone from memory.

The photograph shows a 'Picnic Bus', loaded and about to leave Newstead, date unknown. In the centre is Mrs Willie Mitchell and daughter Annie of Burnfoot Cottage. Pat and Nigel McQueen and second from the right, Tom Bell of the Mill.

Newstead Picnic - Circa 1935.

North Berwick - Bass Rock Boat Trip
Left to Right:
Archie Anderson, Jenny Gill, Alex Anderson, Willie Anderson,
Nellie Anderson, John Cleaver, Alma Brooker.

PROFILE

JIMMY GORDON – PIPER POET

Although born in Dingleton, Jimmy Gordon an uncle of mine, came to live at No. 2 Fortune Row in the early twenties. The row of what was originally three houses, built by the Mein family, was owned by my father.

The rent at that time was £7 per annum, and until the time of his death, this remained unchanged, despite that my father bore the burden of the rates, which were at least double the rent.

A man of many talents, he had been a baker to trade, working in Haddington, but during his time at Newstead, and until his retirement, he was a surfaceman on the railway.

He was a very fine piper and chosen to play a lament at the Melrose War Memorial during the visit of King George V and Queen Mary, when they came to the Borders early in the nineteen twenties.

A considerable achievement was his raising from the Melrose Boy Scouts, a pipe band, teaching both piping and drumming. Among his many pupils were Dr Scott Smith, the Reverend Jack Drummond, Duncan McKinnon and my brother Jack.

A keen ornithologist, he was particularly attracted to what are termed soft billed birds, viz. insectivorous, such as Redstarts, Stone Chats, Whin Chats, Wheaters and the various buntings.

At Newstead he specialised in bee keeping, and was an authority on the Dutch and Italian bee strains, and the dreaded Newcastle disease which wiped out many bee colonies at that time. At one time he had forty hives in his garden.

Another hobby was geese, which he bred, and old English fighting game poultry. Efforts at hybridising them with pheasants however were not a success. The geese were kept in a long field by the bridle path on the Back Road between the railway and the south side of the orchard.

As a taxidermist he mounted all sorts of animals, such as weasels, stoats and squirrels as well as birds of all kinds. One particular rare

Water Rail found dead on the Annay Road, was a prime example. My memories include trapping weasels at a heap of old stones on the Broomhill Road.

He was a song writer, and composed the words and music for "The Lasses of Melrose Toon" and produced many poems on local themes such as "The Ghost of the Bogley Burn" and "The Monster of the River Tweed".

Pipers and whisky however always seem to be inseparable, and although I never recall him to have been under the influence, after his death, and when I acquired the property, it was a surprise when digging in the garden to uncover many half bottles of whisky, presumably buried by him. The bottles of course were empty.

COMPOSED – FRANCE 1917

by

JIMMY GORDON

While daein twa oors sentry go
I often find my mind
wanders back tae happy days
an' scenes o' Auld Lang Syne.
When I was young an' at the schule
mony a happy day
I spent by the side o' Matties burn
that rins by Dingleton Brae.

I wandered fer afield since syne
but never have I seen,
a bonnier place than Melrose
nae maitter where I've been.
There is Gattonsides plantations
shaped like flag, horseshoe and boot
tae view them frae the Eildon Hills
it's grand withoot a doot.

There's Newstead village a bonny place
an' beeches doon the Annay,
tae gie them justice in their praise
I've tried it, but I canna.
But now the place has changed a wee
they've built a lot o' hooses
they're even cleaning oot the wuds
o' tall and bonnie spruces.

Auld customs tae there's fasterns 'een
a thing now o' the past,
an' now the grand old Mason's Walk
is wanin very fast.
The heid yins tae, aboot the place
ye'd think they're in a hurry
tae alter the place as much as they can
sin' it was made a Burgh.

The Melrose folk are no' tae blame
it's strangers come tae bide
that's gien the place the name it has
o' poverty and pride.
Some young yins tae, hae changed their tongue
its a peety they're sae fast
I dinna think I'll alter mine
I'm Melrose tae the last.

GALASHIELS MUSIC FESTIVAL

c.1934

NEWSTEAD VILLAGE DANCERS

Back Left to Right:
Annie Scott, Violet Mitchell, Unknown, Unknown, Helen Scott.

Front Left to Right
Meg Anderson, Unknown, Margaret Douglas, Dorothy Riddell,
Nellie Anderson.

THE RURAL

NEWSTEAD WOMEN'S RURAL INSTITUTE

In the Fairfax Hall c1930

Play – Campbell of Kilmore

Left to Right:
Marie Scott, Janette Scott, Margaret Douglas, Bella McKenzie, Helen Scott,
Meg Anderson, Unknown, Agnes Gordon.

Sitting Front:
Frances Cowie and Belle Gordon.

THE RURAL PARTY

by

Piper Jimmy Gordon

In March we had a party,
Down in the Fairfax hall,
Although we were a trifle packed,
It was much enjoyed by all.

❖   ❖   ❖

Mrs Davie Welcomed all our guests,
who came from far and near,
And hoped they'd have a happy time,
While they were with us here.

❖   ❖   ❖

All enjoyed a lovely tea,
Then it was time to start,
Our programme, every Institute
Doing her little part.

❖   ❖   ❖

Newstead set the ball a-rolling,
With a sketch 'On the 4.15'
The audience laughed so much, we wished
ourselves, we could have seen.

❖   ❖   ❖

Bowland delighted with a song,
Blainslie gave a recitation,
When the W R I ladies meet,
There is no hesitation.

St. Boswells also did a sketch,
As only St. Boswells could,
A lass from Mertoun sat down to play,
But our piano is not so good!

Darnick supplied us with a quiz,
we sure had to use our wits,
Next a recitation from Newtown,
Yes! WRI's have their hits.

The programme finished with a play,
Again, members from our team,
Everyone started laughing,
It really was a scream.

Our President moved votes of thanks,
As also did a member
Of each Institute, for giving them
An evening to remember

We all sang 'God Save Our Queen',
Before going homeward way,
Hoping our guests enjoyed themselves,
And will come again some day.

THE ARTIST – WILLIE HEATLIE

Portrait of the artist.
William Heatlie, from a photograph
by Towert, Edinburgh.

It is scarcely surprising that the beautiful Border Country, with its wealth and variety of subjects, attracted men of artistic tendencies.

So, the region has been favoured by many famous artists, and numerous enthusiasts of lesser merit, who over the years have graced the Newstead neighbourhood. Turner, whose delightful painting of Melrose sat at a spot opposite Newstead, above the famous 'Cowies Hole' pool on the river Tweed. Tom Scott, the famous Selkirk artist, and a member of the Royal Scottish Academy, is believed to have taken lodgings at Newstead, whilst executing his paintings of Newstead Mill and elsewhere.

However, there is one whose works are treasured and popular to this day, with a distinctive Newstead connection and that is of course Willie Heatlie.

Willie Heatlie was born at Ettrick Bridge-End and therefore despite his future Newstead connections, was not a true native of the village. The family moved when Willie was very young to Eildon Hall near Newtown, the residence then of the Duke of Buccleuch, and where Heatlie senior acquired a position as a gardener. Willie had one sister, Isabella who was six years his junior. In his early youth he attended school at Newtown.

Upon the death of his father, who presumably occupied a tied cottage, Mrs Heatlie and her two children found accommodation at a house within the grounds of Melrose Abbey, known as 'Cloisters

Cottage', adjacent to the old Melrose brewery of McLean and Company.

Little seems to be known of his early Melrose contemporaries, or his sojourn at Cloisters, but for some years he studied art in Edinburgh, before returning to Melrose, where his true potential as an artist was to become apparent. His work seems largely to have been water colours, but covered a vast range of delightful subjects, and the suggestion is that his exceptional out put was also for commercial advantage.

Very many village cottages were adorned by Heatlie paintings, depicting local and Border scenery instantly recognisable.

It seems also that he possessed considerable architectural ability as revealed in his many paintings of Melrose Abbey. No doubt he had a prodigious output, as his Abbey productions encompass every aspect, from the Abbey in its entirety, to unusual views and unlikely subjects of pieces of architecture, unappreciated by the casual observer.

When finally Mrs Heatlie died, Willie and Isabella move to St John's Cottage in St John's Wynd in Newstead. This house stood alone, but today many other houses are adjoining it. It appears that Willie had considerably teaching engagements, which encroached on his time, so the output which remains in existence today suggests an exceptional ability. The high quality of his many works however, seems never to have achieved the acclaim accorded to his contemporary local artist Tom Scott.

Despite this overshadowing, Willie Heatlie's work today is highly prized and appreciated the more so by the contemporary nature of the scenes he depicted.

He has been described as a shy, unobtrusive individual, small of stature with black curly hair and a ruddy complexion. It is suspected that he was lacking a robust constitution, as tragically he fell victim to an attack of influenza early in 1892 at the age of forty two.

Of the seven Heatlie's works in my possession today, two are of the Abbey. However, he covered a vast range of subjects. His painting of women drawing water in St John's Wynd, a few feet from his door, is of particular village significance and connection. A reproduction hangs in the Village Hall today.

As the general local opinion was that Willie Heatlie's forte was in water colours, I was surprised to discover in the pictures bequeathed to me, a delightful oil painting dated 1881, when he was twenty three years old. This depicts harvesting by the Gallows Brae in Melrose, with the Gallows trees more prominent than they are today. The trees where highwaymen and other miscreants were hanged, in days gone by are intentionally visible from the Mercat Cross, possibly to satisfy the morbid curiosity such scenes attracted in those harsher days.

So Willie Heatlie's talented interpretations became widely acknowledged and his many works are cherished by owners today. Willie was buried in Melrose cemetery where his many friends erected a memorial stone to his memory.

A story often told, was that some of his paintings became a source of currency and accepted as such, by local traders, on occasions when items of his clothing had to be replaced. He is well worthy of recognition and will not easily be forgotten.

The photo shows St John's Cottage, Newstead, where Willie Heatlie lived and died.

133

PROFILE: SID OVENS

PIGS AND POVERTY

Sid Ovens, his mother, along with his sister Mrs McGinnis and her two sons, Billy and Sandy, arrived in Newstead about 1920 or 1921. They lived in Claymires Cottage. Their background was unknown, but the story was that they had come from South Africa. They were certainly not Rustics, Sid in particular being articulate and well educated.

The rumour then, was that whilst employed either in banking or finance, he had succumbed to temptation or had lost his employment through his propensity for alcohol, which later manifested itself during his long life later in the village.

In some unknown way they acquired also a large stone building formerly housing pigs, at the top of Claymires Lane, and the long strip of land from it eastwards up to Hawthorn Cottage, bounded by the railway and the Back Road. Old Grannie Ovens, Sid's mother, was a dear old soul, and Mrs McGinnis and the boys were sensible and well behaved. Nobody at that time suspected that Sid had a drink problem.

So, with no employment or obvious income, Sid concentrated on breeding pigs, in an amateurish sort of way, eking out their feeding by collecting swill and kitchen scraps from the villagers, potatoes from his strip of land, and turnips purloined from Riddell's turnip fields nearby. The smell from the piggery, especially in hot weather, with the prevailing west wind blowing, disturbed many villagers, even those accustomed to such rustic stock breeding activities.

Sid also ran sweepstakes on all sorts of events, rugby matches, horse racing, the Derby, Grand National and the Boat race, canvassing money around the village.

Presumably after the prize money was paid out he retained a percentage. He likewise drew a source of income providing snippets of Newstead and local news to local papers, as well as assisting farmers, singling turnips, harvesting crops and at the threshing time.

The pigs when mature, were sold at Newton St Boswells stock market. Sid was an outgoing, extrovert, with a pleasant personality, always joking and very popular throughout the village.

However, there was a hidden side, because when funds accrued, Sid would go off on a drinking spree, disappearing for three or four days at a time, only to reappear, craving for more drink, at the various village doors of such villagers that he knew well. Deterring him from persistent efforts he would make to gain access to households, particularly in the early morning, didn't endear him to many. However, in time, all was forgiven, and things would return to normal, until after a lapse of a few months, the process was repeated.

I had an indication of the families' straitened circumstances, when at Christmas time, I was sent by my mother to deliver a present to old Grannie Ovens. She returned the gesture by giving me a small silver spoon, in a blue velvet lined box, not new, but obviously a prized family possession. Even at that early age, the sadness of the situation was obvious to me, and has always remained in my memory.

Sid's nephew, young Sandy McGinnis, was tragically killed flying with the RAF during the war.

There are many memories of Sid Ovens, but one in particular is revealing. Riddell of Townhead Farm, had hired a machine for threshing the corn stacks in the stack yard, and along with others, Sid was recruited to lend a hand. His lot, was the removal of the chaff from the rear of the machine, after the corn had been recovered, a very dirty, dusty job, with no respite until the engine stopped. As a perk, Sid was permitted to take a bag full of chaff as bedding for his pigs. When all was done he filled up a large bag, but as the chaff itself was not heavy, and spying a heap of turnips brought in to feed the cows, slipped, unseen, in with the chaff, some of the turnips for his pigs. Setting out for home all was well, until he reached the brow of the hill, when the bag fell apart, and out came the turnips, in full view rolling down the roadway in the middle of the village, to much amusement but embarrassment for Sid.

Such then was Sid Ovens, although not a native, certainly a village personality. He died in an old people's home at Milfield Jedburgh.

CAPTAIN T A G TULLOH

SUFFERING UNDER THE UNCONSCIOUS "PILATE"

Captain Tulloh occupied Tannachie, just after the end of the 1914-1918 war. Its previous owner was Captain Lang, who was Adjutant of a Battalion of The Kings Own Scottish Borderers, and with his Commanding Officer, went missing at Gallipoli. His name appears on the Newstead War memorial.

The Tulloh's had one son, Gordon, also a Captain. Mrs Tulloh, a rather superior Colonel's lady and calves foot jelly type, didn't fraternise with the villagers. They had an effeminate male cook, called Wattie Morrison, but relied on the villagers for domestic help.

They possessed a pony and trap, the only one in the village, and employed Johnnie Douglas as a groom and coachman. The grounds contained tennis courts, and the field, nowadays the orchard, was grazing for cows, although eventually a cricket pitch was laid out for the benefit of the village boys.

The old Captain was a strongly built, slightly balding man, with a short Hitler type moustache. He obviously had the well being of the village youths as a priority, because one of his first actions was the erection of a large wooden army hut in his field, and the formation of Newstead Village Boys Club.

This became a focal point for us all, especially during the winter months, as it was heated by a stove, and had all manner of gymnastic equipment, including a vaulting horse, as well as all sorts of card games, dominoes, darts etc. We often had boxing matches between the boys, as gloves were provided too.

During the summer we played cricket, but paper chases up to and around the Eildons were great fun, as we took sandwiches and lemonade with us, and had lots of rests. Captain Tulloh also formed a boys' Scout troop, and Cubs, with summer camps at Leaderfoot or nearby. I imagine all expenses were his, as I have no recollection of membership fees.

Concerts, stage plays and magicians were also part of the entertainment. The stage had a trapdoor, and as the hut was built high off the ground, little boys were made to disappear from behind curtains, and reappear when called, at the rear of the hall.

Later, girls were admitted and many came from Melrose. Gilbert and Sullivan operas such as "HMS Pinafore" required a large cast of both sexes.

The spiritual element to all this was Sunday evening Church services taken by Captain Tulloh himself. The High English style however was foreign to most of us, and the chanting of the Creed baffled many of the youngest. Adam (Titch) Mitchell, who died young, was overheard repeating, "suffering under the unconscious Pilate". No doubt Captain Tulloh of Tannachie was a man of vision, and made an impact on Newstead village.

It is sad however, that the ancient name of Tannachie, has been re-named 'The Wells', by transient incomers, with but little thought for the charm and character of the village.

The photgraph shows Captain Tulloh centre, with the Newstead Boys Club. "Cubs" at the club hut in Newstead.

NEWSTEAD BOYS' CLUB

Back Row: Left to Right
John Forrest, Mrs Cowie, John Johnston, Albert Barton, Joe Lawrie.
Second Row: Left to right
Francis Cowie, Netta Purdom, Ella Gill, Annie Mitchell, Tom Fargie,
Mamie Cowie.
Front Row: Left to Right
Kenneth Barton, Alex Forrest, Bill Chapman.

The date of this photograph is uncertain, but it's probably 1933 or 1934. Captain Tulloh was fond of pageantry, and we can only guess what it was about. Empire Day was celebrated in the schools in my day. The characters seem to depict a variety of nationalities, Welsh (Francis Cowie), English (Netta Purdom), Scottish (Annie Mitchell) and the boys appear as Colonials. The flags in the background may be symbolic.

This photograph shows a boys club dance at Earlston in November 1938 with the Founder of the club Captain Gordon Tulloh centre middle row.

Centre Row:
Third from left Bobbie Matheson, on Captain Tulloh's left is Sheila Davidson, Willie Cleaver, unknown, Jack Gordon, and Albert Barton. Behind Captain Tulloh is Alex Forrest.

Club Boys of HMS Pinafore
Willie Cleaver (dark suit, centre of front row), Scott Smith (first left centre
row, with white hat in hand).

VIGNETTES

The many concerts in the Fairfax hall, and Willie Rankine's concert party from Galashiels dressed as pierrots. Meg Hart and her sister from Melrose singing the same old songs, such as, 'Jock O' Hazeldean', 'Coming thro' the Rye' and 'Ca' the Yowes tae the Nowes'

Ca' the yowes tae the nowes
Ca' them whaur the heather grows
Ca' them whaur the burnie rows
My bonnie dearie.

or

Ilka lassie has her laddie
nane they say I
but all the lads they smile at me
when coming thro' the rye.

The Women's Rural Institute, well attended, then popular, and in its heyday. Mrs Davie from Oakendean as president. Baking competitions, whist drives, amateur dramatics ect. Helen Scott, a born actress in a performance of 'Campbell of Kilmore', with my mother as a Scottish soldier, in tunic, kilt and sword.

Mary Davidson's dancing classes of Country and Highland in the school hall, and being criticised for enthusiastically leaping much too high, whilst doing the 'Pas de Bas'.

Bet Barton, surrounded by her large brood on the High Road, pushing the pram, her latest 'Winston' named after Mr Churchill. She, complaining that if you paid all the bills that came in, you would have nothing left over for yourself.

Tom White, searching the village street with a torch on a dark night. When asked what he was looking for, he replied, 'our Tom's swallowed a penny'. Young Tom given a penny and sent up to Bella Scott's shop, had for some reason put it in his mouth and swallowed it.

Myself in sand shoes, leading a large Clydesdale horse to be watered, and on approaching the trough, stupidly allowed the horse to stand on my foot. I had to stand in agony until the horse had quenched its thirst.

Davie Forrest, knocked off the railway embankment by a rabbit. As a railway signalman he was granted permission to catch rabbits on the railway, between Ravenswood junction and Melrose. Having put in a ferret, he was peering into the hole when a rabbit rushed out and connected with his face. He was knocked to the bottom of the bank, in a dazed condition, and gave up his pursuit of rabbits.

OLD VILLAGE NAMES
AND
EXPRESSIONS

BLACK AFFRONTED – This expression mostly used by women meant, ashamed or insulted.

BEN THE HOOSE – Had 'But and Ben' connotations, and referred to the other room in the house.

GLAIKIT – Described someone of limited intelligence, as did also, 'weak in the head' or 'donnert'.

PUGGLED – Being tired.

SCUNNERT – Disgusted or sickened.

BAGGIES – Were minnows caught in the Tweed, by the use of an opened up sugar bag.

HOOLETS – Were owls, and 'Thistecocks' were Willow Wrens.

FOGGIES – Bumble bees, black with white bottoms, brown bees were 'Broonies' and the black with the red rear end 'Red Dockers'. The latter stingless.

ROADS

It seems appropriate to commence this historical chapter with a memory that has haunted me for over seventy five years.

Picture the three sided stone depot by the roadside at the top of the Boat Brae, a long forgotten name, where the road from Newstead moves down hill to the Viaduct. A bleak winter day, a bitter easterly wind, and a bearded ancient squatting on a cold hard stone. His tattered belted overcoat and bonnet, are green with age. His mitten hands wield a hammer to larger stones, to break them into small pieces, just big enough for filling in of pot-holes in the roads. The pathetic little heap, and the arduous heart breaking task, were to earn him a paltry few ha'pence to eke out an existence, as old age pensions were then unknown. The sadness of this scene remains with me to this day.

Another old man was to be seen similarly occupied in the depot by the old bridge over the railway, on the high road to Melrose.

The roads were metalled and rough then as tar macadam only became available about 1922.

The coarse stones were levelled and compressed after watering, by steam rollers. Anyone falling whilst running, or from bicycles, inevitably had skinned bleeding knees and elbows. Such injuries were frequent and common. This applied also to horses, bleeding and damaged animals always distressed me.

Many of the old roads to and from Newstead have gone, altered or been re-routed, so it becomes difficult for someone today to envisage the past. The narrow cart track from Newstead due east towards Ravenswood and the A68 road, was known as Broomhill Road.

The road itself was straight and direct, with a side roadway leading southwards to Broomhill Farm. The principal route emerged on the A68, opposite the Ravenswood North Gate Lodge, but it no longer exists today.

Midway between this lodge and Leaderfoot bridge, stood an unusual elaborate, stone built, watering place for horses and cattle, sheep and humans. Two low side tubs allowed for sheep to drink,

143

whilst the centre was long and wide to accommodate several horses or cattle at a time. A large iron drinking cup, secured by an iron chain was available for pedestrians and thirsty travellers, this supply being independent from the animal source of water.

The water emerged from a natural spring, and was always pure, cold and delicious to drink.

Another nearby watering point, but less elaborate, and smaller, was located in the wall at the foot of Gledswood Brae, close by the game keeper's cottage and the narrow humped backed bridge over the Leader. It could accommodate horses, and it also had an iron chained drinking cup.

We have lost too many of the old fashioned roads, and also some bridges too. The well known, and familiar humped backed bridge over the railway had character and style, on the High road to Melrose passing the Tub Nursery. Who remembers it now?

The closing to traffic of the Leaderfoot and Bogley Burn roads at least provides a blissful interlude from the by-pass hustle and bustle; and the Eildon Tree Wishing Stone of our youthful days is available once again.

Milestones, almost unknown today, were a common feature on the roads and a helpful assistance to travellers. One unusual and exceptional one stood on the main road near the watering place between Ravenswood North Gate Lodge, and the road bridge over the Tweed.

The stone had a domed top and the distance was recorded in Roman numerals. It had the words EBOR and PEDES on each side. Both are of Roman or Latin origin. Ebor was known to be the Roman name for York, and Pedes meant feet, or footsteps.

It was sited, not at road level, but on the embankment, and was frequently obscured by foliage, so passed unnoticed on most occasions. To my knowledge it existed in the early twenties, but perhaps with the language being unfamiliar to the natives it seems to have been treated with indifference and neglect. Liz Taylor however, recalls seeing it still on the roadside in the 1940's.

Its proximity to the Roman fort suggests an ancient Roman connection, and the Roman numerals and lettering add weight to this theory.

Its disappearance remains a mystery but extensive road works and alterations in recent years may have some bearing on this.

Certainly another ancient historic treasure has been lost, yet again!

Beryl, with a young Barbara, near the Roman milestone at Ravenswood, with the unusual watering trough and Leaderfoot viaduct seen through the trees in the background.

PROFILE – BOB ANDERSON

The Andersons lived in the centre of the three houses then in Back Road, at Newstead. All were built by the Pringles, in a traditional style and very similar. 'Roselea' was however distinguished by the ornamentation of its gateway. The pillars were decorated by a large stone carved thistle on one side, and a rose on the other. They seemed much more suited to a baronial hall and their origin was obscure.

Bob Anderson was a boot maker by trade and employed by Robertson the Bootmaker in the Market Square Melrose. The family grew rapidly over the years and additional lean-to buildings were necessarily added to the house to accommodate the fifteen offspring and their parents.

In an effort to provide for this large family, Bob gave up work at Robertson's, and having erected a large wooden shed in the garden, decided to go into business on his own account.

The clients were mainly villagers, and leather boots and shoes were the norm, so there was always work available. He augmented this daily income by taking the night time duty of village gas lighter, for the Melrose Gas Company.

The gas was manufactured at the Melrose Gas Works, which stood at the entrance to Melrose school, and was largely owned by the Curle family.

Newstead had only a very few gas street lamps, but Bob, with his long pole, activated the lights both off and on twice each night. The lamps were never allowed to be on throughout the night as they are today.

The Andersons were an enterprising family. Young Bob the eldest son emigrated to Canada, and Lawrence to New Zealand. Others were accomplished, but self-taught, musicians and formed an accordion band, playing at dances and concerts.

At that time a foot path bordered the Back Roadway from Riddell's farm to the houses, and the family made great efforts to maintain it and keep it clean and tidy. The Well Roadie, from the Back

Road to the main road, was also in constant use.

There was always much amusement when the local baker arrived with his bread deliveries to the village, as Mrs Anderson's supply of loaves for the family, filled a large wicker clothes basket.

Unhappily the boot making trade declined, and the numerous Andersons dispersed, so none remain in the village today.

The magnificent and unusual gateway was found unsuitable and unacceptable to new occupants, so today there is no longer a trace of Newstead's largest ever family, the Andersons.

LIBRARY COTTAGE

Old Willie Clark and his wife occupied, as caretakers, Library Cottage in St John's Wynd, part of the Fairfax bequest to the village. A joiner to trade, he had come to Newstead from Leaderfoot. I believe they were the first caretakers, but the library or its existence was never part of village conversation to my knowledge, nor was there any apparent enthusiasm for recreational reading. The villagers probably had other things on their minds.

The house was divided into two compartments, and according to Willie Cleaver, their grandson who I have consulted, the Wynd end of the house was never used in their time, or very seldom. He said that he seemed to recall seeing books, but couldn't swear to it, but remembers an old lamp lit chandelier in the centre of the ceiling, with one or two larger lamps providing reading light. The chandelier had a mechanism whereby it could be lowered, to light, clean the glass or refill with paraffin.

Willie Clark and his wife lived in the other end, where there was a sink by the window on the Roadside, and a brass double bed against the back wall. An old grandfather clock stood between the library and their living quarters. The clock is now in Los Angeles where Willie Cleaver now lives.

It does seem at least to have been inconvenient for intending readers to gain access to the library. The only access to Library Cottage was by the wooden door in St John's Wynd, and the surrounding high wall was then unbroken.

Old Willie, was inclined to be ill tempered and his village nickname became "Wicked Willie". His ill temper probably related to the fact that after forty years of residence in the village, and having come from afar as Leaderfoot he was still classed as an incomer!

BOGLEY BURN

With the advent of the Melrose bypass and the closure of the Bogley Burn road between Melrose and Newtown, it would be sad if its historical legendary associations were to be diminished.

Long a focus of Border folklore with its bogles, witches, ghosts etc., it has also attracted the attention of local poets (not to mention that Thomas the Rhymer met the Queen of the Fairies there too).

However, my recollections are of it as a drove road for cattle and sheep.

Melrose butchers Dod Bunyan and Davie Sanderson bought livestock at Newtown market, which were herded on foot from Newtown up the Bogley to its junction with the Banks Road from Newstead.

The route was then downhill towards Newstead, emerging at Newstead Mill, then along the Annay Road to the slaughterhouse near Melrose.

This exercise was often fraught with excitement at the Newstead end, and controlling animals at the various road junctions often became a problem. Davie Sanderson, of course, was the scrum-half in Ned Haig's original Melrose Sevens team, when Ned Haig invented the Rugby Seven-a-Side game.

At that time large parties of American tourists arrived by train at Melrose station, to tour the Scott Country. They were met by horse-drawn cabs and conveyed to three hotels – the George and Abbotsford, the Abbey Hotel (now demolished) and the Waverley Hydro.

The first day comprised a journey over the Bogley Burn through St Boswells to Dryburgh Abbey, then on to Scott's View, returning via Leaderfoot and through Newstead.

On the second day, Abbotsford itself was visited, before departure on the third.

The conveyances were horse-drawn and referred to as charabancs, being open topped with very high seating for about twelve persons or more. They caused quite a stir and excitement passing through the village, in convoy.

One day a cabbie by the name of Joe Snowie took a party of Americans over the Bogley Burn road. On reaching the summit, with the Eildon Hills in view, one of the passengers turned to Snowie and asked if there were any wild animals in those parts.

Snowie replied in the negative. The American then said; "What are there no foxes or badgers here"? "Oh", replied Snowie, "I thought you meant lions and tigers!".

The Bogley pre-war proved a useful route when members of the royal family were guests of the Duke of Buccleuch at Eildon Hall, allowing them to join the late Pullman train to London at Melrose station.

Such a pity that the old Bogley Burn connections are now abandoned.

THE GIANT OF BOGLEY BURN

by

Piper Jamie Gordon

Yin nicht as I was wandering west
Weel primed wi Mrs Brydon's best,
and riftin fu' richt up to here wi
Roderic's Dhu and Sale Ring Beer.

❖   ❖   ❖

It was a sale day at Newtoon, and
just as usual I'd gaen doon;
I'd got a guid price for my sheep,
but I had drank not wisely, but too well
so hence tae you this tale I tell.

❖   ❖   ❖

What though the road be drear and long,
This nicht tae Melrose I maun gang,
I tak the road in sic a state, the
nicht is dark, the oor is late.

❖   ❖   ❖

Wi' shufflin gait and senses reelin,
Thro railway arch my way I'm feelin,
Wi' a my facalties bereft, I pass the
Sale-room on my left.

❖   ❖   ❖

Wi' thochts o' warlocks in my mind,
The cottages are left behind;
I whustled owre an auld scotch sonnet
Tae keep the bees oot o' ma bonnet.

❖   ❖   ❖

The wind was whustlin in the wuds,
The wind came glintin thro' the cluds,
when tae my relief, I saw, the big white
gates o' Eildon Ha'.

I stoppit here tae ha' a blaw,
I hadnae done sae bad at a',
But ae the thocht gaed me a turn,
I'd yet to cross the Bogley Burn,
and longer here I couldna stay, so
of again up Eildon Brae.

When I got tae the tap and swung
round the bend,
By the long shears o' Gordon, my
hair it stood on end.

Ma hairt intae ma breeks it sank,
for there a giant sat on the bank,
and sic a giant was never seen,
The great Goliath must have been,
a dwarf compared in each dimention,
for this yin passed a' comprehension.

His heid was the size o' three, a
cudgel lay across his knee,
His hair was long and hung in rapes,
his hands they were like tattie graips,
his arms were baith long and teuch,
his legs were danglin in the seuch.

I couldna turn, I couldna move, me onward
something seemed to shove,
I was frozen tae the very bone, but ae
that something drew me on.

A substance present, yet not real that
draws like magnet intae steel,
or like the bonnie lark that rises,
the wily weasel hypnotises, or like
the butterfly so bright, by instinct
always flies to light.

Each time I looked I saw him clearer,
he drew me nearer, ever nearer
Until I stood before him quakin,
Ma braith cam hard ma knees were shakin.

I thoght my end was very near,
I must have wet ma breeks wi' fear.
His head it shot oot in trice, and
gripped me as in a vice.

He squeezed me till I thocht he'd broke it,
The bottle in ma tapcoat pocket,
He squeezed me till ma ribs did crack,
and ground his teeth but never spak,
and some strange thought it may seem to be,
Somehow, he'd left ma airm free.

Though fu' ma brain was working quick,
I grippit hard ma guid ash stick,
I gaid ma stick a michty swing, and
brought it doon wi' sic a ding,
As with a thud richt hard it fell,
his heid exploded like a shell.

And then my God, mang smoke and din,
three heids sprang up insteed o' yin,
wi' faces grinnin and uncouth, blue
flames cam flamin oot his mooth.

The heat was great, it singed ma hair,
and smell o' brimstone filled the air,
how it was done I ne'er could tell,
I struggled free and ran like hell.

Richt doon the brae and thro' the burn
and never yince ma heid did turn,
loud roars and shouts the air was fillin,
the brae was steep the pace was killin,
I wad put tae shame yire racin wunners.

I thocht ma very legs wud snap, but while
ye cough, I reached the tap,
I stretched ma legs wi' a ma poor,
you couldna see ma arse for stoor.

Sic rinnin ne'er was ever seen, as I
flew on past Oakendean, but then the pace
began tae tell I couped ma fit and doon I fell.

Then up and gaed ma knees a rub, and of
again richt past the Tub,
Wi' frichtsome thochts ma brain it
reeled, as I drew up at Riddles field.

I stoppit here for jist a bit, for rinnin mair I wasna fit,
Then staggerin on as best I could,
I reached the gates o' Prior's Wood, and
here, ma heated brain tae cool, I dooked
ma heid in tinnies pool.

This nicht I'd got in tae disgrace,
I'd yet a ragin wife tae face,
and sic a bitch she devil tak us,
was kenned tween Hawick and Longformacus.

Some wear the breeks, she wears the buits,
her tongue it would hae clippit cloots,
God help the puir man that should hae
another wife like Jean Guthrae.

Refreshed a bit, though sair and lame,
I took the road and made for hame,
but in the dark I lost masel, and
wandered in by "Wullies Well".

The Maut Hoose burn was rinnin fu'
the nicht it aye the darker grew,
Ma feet I couldnae langer keep, and
sittin doon, I fell asleep.

When I awoke, ma heid was splittin,
a' mixed up like a plooman's flittin,
At "Wullies Well" I cooled ma brain,
and vowed I'd ne'er touch drink again.

Tak ma advice wha read this tale, and
e'er should gang tae Newtoon sale.
If Brydons Whuskey hoves yer wame,
be shair ye catch the last train hame.

When tae "strong drink" ye tak a turn,
Aye mind "The Giant o' Bogley Burn".

LANDMARKS

GONE BUT NOT FORGOTTEN

In old age, ever present and dominating nostalgic memories are probably an unhealthy condition, but as the ageing process proceeds in its inevitable way, there is often an involuntary reaction to current, prevailing situations over which we have no obvious control. Often those are destructive, or detracting from images, held dearly, of life and fond memories of times gone by.

The old Newstead which we knew so well, apparently unchanged for centuries and which we believed to be framed in time, has, even in my lifetime, suffered irreversible environmental damage. The sense of despair is overwhelming.

Gone are the spectacular lines of the massive great beeches lining the Middle Walk to Melrose, and on the Annay Road. The ash trees on both sides of the High Road all the way to Melrose, and the solitary beech on the brow of the hill, the scene of a notorious attempted rape of a Newstead girl, have likewise disappeared. The great plane tree at the top of St John's Wynd, was also felled without permission. Plane Tree Cottage bears its name today.

Another long row of thirteen ancient trees on the Back Road, a haven for owls, woodpeckers, jackdaws and much other wild life, were all felled in one day, in a fit of pique when new residents claimed overhanging branches on the road were dangerous and threatened legal action against the aged owner.

Of many old buildings there is today no trace. Gone is the Mill, the Boy's Club in Tannachie grounds, Willie Slater's two storied house at the bottom of Claymires Lane, where as boys we searched for swallows and other birds nests, are all now just memories.

The Double House at the corner leading to the Yiddy, housing Johnny Cathrae on the top and Donald McRitchie below, is now a green area, seldom used by villagers. The marvellous Fairfax Hall and Fairfax Cottage, the caretakers house by the entrance gates, are no more, as is the stone stairway from the top floor of the Auld Hoose, then exiting on to the Main Street. The large lodging house between the Auld Hoose and Briar Cottage has been substituted by four modern dwellings. Wat Tait's in St John's Wynd and the Hardies' thatched cottage are derelict. Riddell's Town Head farm and Ford's Barnet farm are both abandoned and no longer active village elements.

Depressing it may be, but old memories are retained and fortunately cannot be entirely eliminated.

TOPOGRAPHY

The charm and character of the old Newstead village, has alas, been destroyed in very recent years by some abysmal decisions of various planners, and all in the name of conservation. The villagers of today seem oblivious, but such is the nature of the times. The much hyped pretence of conservation as depicted today, is innocuous and futile.

In my lifetime alone, Newstead has lost fourteen old houses, various stables and ancient walls and wells. The Mill has gone, as has the old Fairfax Hall. The delightful old local hospital has been transformed into offices, with modern architectural blocks added, but greatly to the detriment of its appearance. By contrast, new housing and developments number a staggering fifty four, with twelve more awaiting approval, and unspecified numbers due eventually in the Orchard site.

In addition, at least one hundred and fifty magnificent Beech, Elm, Ash and Lime trees, many centuries old, have been felled. No re-planting seems to have been contemplated. Newstead has been denuded all to its detriment. How has this come about? It seems easy to fault the applicants, but approval and supervision of plans, remains the duty of the Planning Authority. Ours however, would seem to have had, over recent years, a certain lack of vision, or perception, if not competence.

How else can this be, when one examines the many recent additions to the village, which bear no resemblance to, nor are in keeping with, the original styles of this ancient urban village. Add to this, an ineffective Village Conservation organisation, and a toothless Local Community Council and the recipe is complete.

Despite all the obvious signs, the current theme emblazoned on every occasion, is conservation. A misnomer indeed!

A NEWSTEAD SWAN SONG

A distinctive feature of the Newstead houses of old, was that they were purposely sited to face south, were enclosed by very high, well built walls against the prevailing winds, and almost every garden contained fruit trees of some sort.

So-called developers of today, appear to consider a southern aspect of little importance, nor do the occupying populace seem to appreciate, or perceive its advantages. Dwellings erected today seldom feature natural stone and boundary divisions, if they exist, are corralled in wooden enclosures more suited to an agricultural scene.

Contrast this with our Masonic stonework inheritance, still in existence in Newstead today, and in apparently, mundane, everyday surroundings, all of some style, and high quality workmanship. The old byre on the Yiddy Road, and the distinctive stonework with unusual wall finishing or the ancient abandoned well, set and moulded into the contours of the wall in the 'Wall Roadie' Right of Way; or the old steading in St John's Wynd, again featuring particularly fine stone work, and rounded corners of great charm, are particularly fine examples.

Townhead Farm Creamery, and the exceptionally high wall enclosing the orchard, are village features which must be preserved. Sadly, many ancient walls, truly works of art, which have existed for centuries, have been removed or destroyed by unthinking adventurers in recent years.

The Planning Authorities, supposedly guardians of our heritage, fail us at every turn.

I have long since despaired at the rapid deterioration today of the old village, but still rejoice that memories of the wonderful scenes of long ago, are retained and can never be eradicated completely.

IT'S ME!

The exclamatory introduction when my daughter 'phones from afar.

So, a Valentine for dear Mother on 14th February 1916, and the Chinese year of the Dragon, should, one would assume, qualify as something quite special. Alas it was not to be.

Although born at Fortune Row, a fortune has escaped me, so with massive inhibitions and devoid of all ambitions, my earthly progress through life, has been guided by chance, Good Luck or perhaps a Deity. How else does one explain the pleasure life has given me? Add a devoted loving wife, and daughter, allied to some truly faithful friends and life would appear complete, shielding us apparently from crisis and tragedy.

Perhaps there is still a price to be paid. I have always loved old Newstead, and as my wife has often proclaimed, I might just still be lucky to die at dear old Fortune Row and the house I was born in.

This being "Me", I must be permitted a final story.

I was married in India at Delhi in 1945, and in making preparations, was naturally in communications with my fiancée and prospective spouse. She was stationed as a Nursing Sister in the Army, many miles away in the south of India at Deolali or Nasik, near to Bombay.

"Deolali Tap" was a well known British Army term for an expatriate type of drink or disease induced madness.

Arrangements for our marriage had been finalised, so I despatched, through the Indian Posts and Telegraph system, a telegram confirming that all was well. With some confidence and a casual knowledge of Urdu, and assuming it would be understood, I ended the message with the common expression, "*thik hai*". This means literally, everything is o.k., or all is well.

The Indian Babu, or clerk, observing the message to be in the English language, either out of malice, or fun, assumed that the text was incomplete and added the letter 'c' before the 'k' in thik, and 'r' after the 'i' in hai. The resulting telegram arrived with the final ending, "everything thick hair".

When queried by the recipient, I had no explanation but only considerable embarrassment.

In retrospect it seems slightly amusing. Things always happened to "Me".

OLD SCOTS SONG

JIM GORDON'S PARTY PIECE

When first I met my Jean
She was only seventeen
That's the age they say, sae pretty and sae sweet
In my eyes she'as nae' a fault
Tho' she walks with a wee bit halt
For the want o' ony insteps tae her feet.

❖　　❖　　❖

Chorus: Jean, Jean my bonnie lassie Jean
Come to my arms once again
And tho' they sae your feet are flat
You're nane the waur o' that
You're my ane bonnie Scots lassie Jean.

❖　　❖　　❖

On the night that I proposed
Jeannie's mother sat and dosed
By the fireside in her auld accustomed seat
But my Jeannie stood upricht
She was in an awfu' fricht
That I'd take a scunner at her feet.

❖　　❖　　❖

Chorus

❖　　❖　　❖

Twas in Edinburgh toon
That we spent our honeymoon
And we went to get our photos' took in state
The photographer said it must not be
A full length but a bust for I canna
Get your feet into the plate.

Chorus

Oh the streets were mud and glaur
So we took a tramway car
Just to get a wee bit hurl along the street
But the conductor said my lass
If I'm going to let ye pass
Ye maun tak another ticket for your feet.

Chorus

Noo my Jeannies' old and worn
And her wedding dress is torn
Into pieces for to make the bairnies neat
But this I'm telling you
If your lass is good and true
Just ye mauna care a damn about her feet.

Final Chorus.

Last verse, slower tempo

THE ROMAN FORT – NEWSTEAD

General Plan of the Site

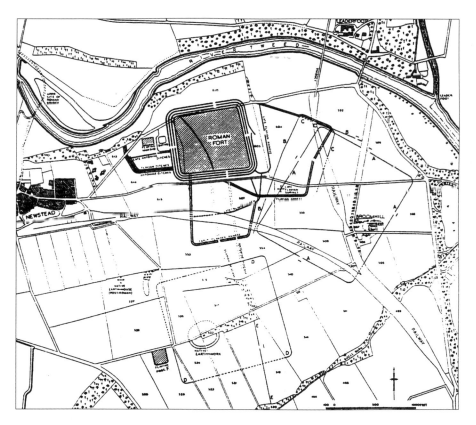

The Roman fort lies on a high plateau overlooking the Tweed. No crossing of the river would have been possible in its vicinity, due to the cliffs, and it would appear that Dere Street crossed the river somewhere near the ford above the Boiler pool.

Note the Yiddy road leads from Newstead towards the approximate site of the Roman bridge below Kittyfield.

SOME NEWSTEAD TREASURES

Both the altars shown are lodged in the National Museum of Antiquities in Edinburgh.

    The altar shown on the left was found in a well. It reads "To Jupiter, best and greatest, Gaius Arrius Domitianus Centurion of the Twentieth Legion Valeria Victrix has paid his vow, willingly, gladly and deservedly".

    The right hand altar was found in 1910. It reads "To Apollo, Lucius Maximus Gaetulius Centurion of the Legion".

POACHERS AND POACHING

Immediately after the first world war in the country and the Borders, living conditions were hard indeed, with employment difficult to achieve.

The vast numbers of returned soldiers, many without limbs or blinded, selling matches on street corners or begging, was a common and depressing sight. The many too, who just did not return left affected families generally grieving and depressed.

So the atmosphere then was unhappy, and sustaining large families on low incomes was a major problem for many villagers. Native game such as rabbits, pheasants, ducks, pigeons and partridges were prolific. Rabbits had reached plague proportions and salmon in the river Tweed abounded to the extent that it was common for us youngsters to go as far as Selkirk and Mertoun not to mention Melrose Caulds, to marvel and view the progress of salmon leaping and working their way up stream to spawn and breed in the thousands. All the large local estates such as Drygrange, Gledswood and Ravenswood had game keepers, but no artificial breeding of pheasants was necessary.

Farming husbandry in those days was less sophisticated and harvesting was at times wasteful. The fields generally were small and divided by many hedges giving refuge to much wild life. The practice of threshing grain in the fields as opposed to in the farm steading provided seeds and winter sustenance for a large variety of native birds and game species.

So the area provided an over abundance of game, jealously claimed by the landowners, and the law supported them when anyone attempted to take rabbits, or other game with out permission. It seems ironic that despite the rabbit plague and the destruction caused to crops, it was felt necessary to take to court anyone caught in the act of catching these rabbits.

Poaching seems an unpleasant and inappropriate word. However the locals, either out of necessity or bravado were undeterred and poaching, salmon particularly, as well as rabbits almost endemic.

The most unlikely characters indulged in different ways. Gun laws seem to have been less restricted as individuals with no agricultural or equivalent connections possessed shotguns. Pheasants silhouetted roosting in trees at night were easy prey. Rabbits could be snared, shot or caught in nets after Ferreting.

Some men made a living trapping rabbits to order, and bicycles festooned with dead rabbits in pairs, with legs threaded together were a popular sight. Rabbit too was a common source of food in many houses, and not considered degrading in those days. Ducks could be caught in gin traps under water with grain or corn as bait, drowning the ducks when activated.

Salmon of course being so abundant, palatable and comparatively easy to obtain, became the focus of many poachers, amateur and professional, so a perpetual conflict with water bailiffs and Police existed.

My early recollections when very, very young, was a gathering of men, including Andersons and Mitchells from the village, on the Battery Dyke observing salmon spawning in the river Tweed. One man had a rake hook which resembles a gardeners rake with five or six iron hooked fingers attached to a length of rope. The rake is swung around to gain momentum and propelled through the air to descend on the river bed on the offside of the salmon. When in position a sharp tug on the rope resulted in the barbed hooks being imbedded in the fish's flanks. On this day the thrower or poacher was successful, as he ran off down stream following the reaction of the fish.

This was the first and only time I have observed this implement in use. They are however preserved in some local museums. Many people poached salmon.

It was common for a stranger to arrive knocking on a door at night offering fish at a cheap price. My dear Mother was always of the opinion, in declining when this happened to her, that perhaps the fish were diseased. This fungus on salmon is still prevalent today. So unscrupulous men it seems caught such ill specimens and through dragging them through grass, removed the unsightly appearance. For some reason we were a fastidious family. Hygiene being a high priority. Fortunately it still exists and colours my outlook today.

The revealing extent of poaching encompassed even the school boys. I remember during a lunchtime interval at Melrose school, watching a contemporary class mate Ikey Stuart, hooking salmon above the Melrose Cauld, at a spot below the bowling green. Sadly Ikey was accidentally to drown at Darnick, when bathing in the Tweed.

An amusing incident to emphasise how widespread salmon poaching prevailed, occurred at the East Port, Melrose, where various old established Melrose families lived. Mrs Crawford went shopping, pushing young Adam Crawford in an old fashioned pram. Mrs Allen, who met her, stopped and spoke, eyed under the pram balanced on the axles, a short rod and salmon cleek. She, jokingly remarked "are you off poaching again?" Mrs Crawford was suitably embarrassed when the cleek was pointed out to her. It appeared that old Jock Crawford, Adam's father, who was a baker with Geordie Wallace, had returned the previous night from a salmon poaching expedition, and lodged the rod and cleek under the pram in the hallway.

Jock Pringle also lived in the East Port, before he came to Newstead's Back Road, and he too was a notorious poacher, disposing of his catches mainly at the Ship Inn. On another occasion Jock arrived home proudly showing off an otter which he had somehow caught and killed, triumphantly showing it off to old Mr Cleghorn, nicknamed Cleggie, who lived in the flat below. Cleggie was an odd effeminate type who rouged his cheeks, so was the focus of much merriment. Amid the jollifications, the otter which had only really been stunned, came to life. Everyone became alarmed at this, until Jock grabbed it by the tail and crashing its head on the floor, with blood bespattering the wall paper and linoleum, much to Mrs Pringle's fury and anger.

Other methods of salmon poaching involved the use of nets, and what was known as "Burning the Water" during which torches or lights on the river at night were sufficient to lure the fish.

Drygrange Estate encompassed the Newstead area, and the head gamekeeper Mr McLean was obviously well known to the local poaching fraternity. Neither my family, or myself were ever involved in poaching, but my interest as a naturalist has been preserved.

Very many years later, in Central Africa at Kisumu on the shores of lake Victoria, I was a guest at a Caledonian Society Dinner. One of the members all Scottish of course, recited a poem which I have always remembered, and now seems appropriate. It concerned an article in the South African press, headlined "Two Men were Fined £120 a Piece for Poaching a White Rhinoceros".

> I've poached a pickle paitricks when the leaves wer turnin' sere
> I've poached a twa-three hares an' grouse and maybe whiles a deer
> But ow, it sems an uncothing an' just a wee mysterious
> Hoo any mortal could contrive to poach a rhinocerious
>
> I've crackit wi' the keeper, pockets packed wi' pheasants eggs
> An' ten-pun saumon hangin' doun in baith my trowser legs
> But eh, I doot effects wud be a wee thing deleterious
> Gin ye shuld stow intil yer brecks a brace o' rhinocerious.
>
> I mind hoo me an' Wullie shot a Royal in Braemar
> An' brocht him doun tae Atholl by the licht o' mune an' star
> An' eh sirs but the canny beast contrived to fash an' weary us –
> Yey staigs maun be but bairns play beside a rhinocerious.
>
> I thocht I kent o' poachin' jist as muckle's ither men
> But there is still a tw-three things I doot I dinna ken
> An' noo I cannot rest, my brain is growin' that delerious
> Tae win awa tae Africa an' poach a rhinocerious.

Poaching does seem to have been great fun!

BIRD SHOWS

The British love of pets is generally acknowledged and accepted. Today dogs and cats predominate. However, eighty years ago in the Border area things were very different.

Certainly nearly every household kept a pet or pets, but the range and variety when viewed in retrospect was astonishing. They included caged birds for singing or exhibition, rabbits, guinea pigs, ornamental pigeons and turtle doves, bantams, fancy mice, owls, squirrels, jackdaws, exotic foreign pheasants, as well as unusual dogs such as Borzois or St Bernard's. Cats were also used for exhibition purposes. All this, and the sheer variety inclined and induced a necessity for competition and showing, much in decline today and almost forgotten.

Every major town held a Bird Show annually, which included classes for all the aforementioned species as well as Poultry and Ducks.

In some instances bird keeping acquired a business aspect. The 'Buckmaster Bill', the original Bill introduced by Lord Buckmaster, for the protection of birds had not yet been passed. Many individuals were engaged in trapping wild birds for a living, particularly Bullfinches, Goldfinches, Linnets, and Greenfinches , which in those days were prolific. Dozens of such birds were caught and sent off by train to dealers in the South.

It was a common sight to see a bird cage hanging on the wall of a cottage outside in the summer, and the bird in full of song.

Many bird enthusiasts, normally known then as fanciers, concentrated on breeding canaries of which there was a large variety, many, sadly not available today. They included breeds such as Norwich, Border, Yorkshire, Scots Fancy, Lizards and Crests.

All were common and competition at the bird shows was keen, with much rivalry and deviousness between breeders was a common feature. Some, if they had money, would buy in birds from English sources or champions, and previous winners, if they were unable to breed suitable birds themselves. Apart from the prestige of being a winner, the prize money, cups, medals and numerous special prizes donated by local traders was considerable. Suit lengths, cardigans, legs of smoked ham and a whole variety of merchandise relating to the donors business were available to be won.

Beside canaries, there was a section for British birds of all kinds. These had been caught in the woods or hills and ranged from all the seed eaters such as Goldfinch, Bullfinch, Siskin, Redpoll, Linnet, Hawfinch, Crossbill, Chaffinch, Bramblefinch, Twite, to hybrids of the same species. The insectivorous birds known as softbills also comprised a huge variety, including Whinchats, Wheateaters, Redstarts both black and red, Stonechats, Blackbirds, Thrushes and Mistle Thrushes.

There was again much skulduggery and cheating in the exhibition of British birds. Feathers could be removed, or the birds subjected to colour enhancement by spraying with dye. The continental Goldfinches and Bullfinches are larger and more colourful than their British counterparts so this was also exploited by some unscrupulous individuals.

It was possible at that time to purchase from bird dealers, what was described as a 'Stick' of Siberian Goldfinches. This came with twelve small wicker cages each containing a bird, the whole being fastened to and held on a short piece of wood. These birds were often shown and exhibited in the British bird classes and were frequently successful in deceiving the judges.

The Bird Shows also catered for rabbits, which likewise included a large range of varieties not seen today. Chinchillas, English, Belgian Hares, Havanas, Lops, Dutch, Flemish Giants and Angoras, and many others. The Havanas were a dark chocolate colour, the Lops had extremely long ears and the Dutch were half black and half white, very similar to Belted Galloway cattle, which we can see today.

Guinea pigs also appeared at Bird Shows. They came in an array of different colours. English were smooth coated, but Peruvians had extremely long hair which required combing and brushing. Abyssinians had coats of rosetted hair which was a feature of excellence for exhibition, and Dutch were again mostly of the black and white variety.

Fancy mice were also a popular feature at some Bird Shows. They came in all colours. The judges handled mice by grasping the tail at its base. If this was not done correctly the skin could easily break off exposing the bone. It often surprised me that no judge ever appeared to get bitten in the process.

Many fanciers concentrated on pigeons, and again many varieties were on display, which are unavailable today. Pouters, Turbots, Nuns, Tumblers, Fantails and Modenas, were all common and came in a vast range of colour. Racing pigeons too provided large classes.

Poultry, Bantams and Ducks also added to the interest in local bird shows, and also embraced a wide variety of breeds. Light Sussex, Rhode Island Red, Anconas, Barred Rocks, white and black Leghorns, Wyandottes, blue Andelusians, Old English Game, Spangles and Silkies were all prominent features as well as a variety of ornamental pheasants, Golden, Silver, Lady Amhersts and many others. Ducks were for the most part, Khaki Campbell, Aylesbury, Indian Runners and Muscovy.

The few Bird Shows today, have a predominance of budgerigars, in a huge variety of colours. They are also popular as pets for many old grannies. It is remarkable that when I was young the budgerigar, an Australian parakeet being introduced to this country was entirely green in colour. The standard nest for breeding was a coconut husk.

It really is astonishing how man's ingenuity allied to intensive breeding of budgies seems to have eclipsed natural evolution in producing such a range of colours, and in such a short space of time.

Pets in the old days led much more natural lives, and dogs and cats fared well enough on household scraps, bones from the butchers etc. augmented by an abundance of rabbits. Tinned pet food was unknown.

We also lived in an era when the veterinary profession was confined to farm animals. Unfortunately today the vet's influences encompass a vast range from old grannies budgie to a variety of domestic animals with the treatment of dogs and cats a most lucrative source of income, seemingly unregulated. The enormous bills for the necessary treatments are a constant source of discussion and resentment amongst pet owners today.

However, the Bird Shows I most remember were held in Peebles, Innerleithen, Hawick, Galashiels, Selkirk, Duns and of course Melrose. In Melrose the Corn Exchange was always the venue. Sam Rainey whose mother ran the bus office in Abbey Street in Melrose, and who himself was a bus driver in those early days, was a canny slow talking soul, who bred and exhibited Border Fancy Canaries. Another Border canary amateur was old Jimmy Allan, locally known as Bowie, who was a railway surfaceman from the East Port in Melrose.

On one occasion at a Bird Show in the Corn Exchange they were both exhibiting birds. On the stage Jimmy encountered Sam and as they proceeded to examine the various merits of the birds, Jimmy asked Sam what he thought of his birds. After some deliberation Sam gave his opinion that it was a nice specimen but, 'Gie weak in the heid'! At that old Bowie exploded with the remark, 'Dem tae hell you're weak in the heid'!

Such was the competitive style in those faraway days, and the demise of such bird keeping interest is attributed by some to the high cost of bird seed today.

So we oldies in Newstead look back with a nostalgic longing for the return of many lost species, and a type of lifestyle and hobbies which have largely disappeared.

Have we really seen the best days?

This photograph taken many years ago at a Bird Show in Kelso shows an old Newstead fancier, John Gordon – my father – with his prizewinners.

GLIMPSES

In recounting old memories of village life, problems arise from at least two sources. The oldest and first recollections, and the intervening additional experiences. In the growing up years, newcomers to the village seem to intrude into the original equation. So, while the inclusion of the former is imperative, subsequent additions of more recent historical significance tend to confuse us, and therefore defuse the original conception.

A historical observation, if it is to succeed, requires a clear definition. With this in mind it seems timely to produce some pen pictures of other old but less illustrious villagers of those times. They all occupied a place in old Newstead eighty years ago, and deserve a mention.

Many however were not necessarily born in Newstead. To be truly native born was, in the eyes of many, a type of proud accolade, so when insults were exchanged, or behavioural patterns challenged, the derogatory term "incomer" was applied. This has prevailed over many years and continues even today. It is naturally much resented. Some of the following characters fell into the "Incomer" category.

JOHNNY GIBSON

Johnny Gibson lived in the last house at the top of Claymires Lane. It was called Hazeldean Cottage at that time, and thought to be a Gate Lodge for Hazeldean House. The house name however has been changed by individual owners over recent years. Johnny was a plumber by trade. He suffered and struggled continuously with ulcers of the stomach, constantly appearing at house doors begging for baking soda. This had anti-acid properties and gave some relief.

Home baking was a necessary feature of house keeping in the early days, so it was freely available. The usual method of dispensing was directly into Johnny's open hand, thence into his mouth, dry, and without the benefit of water to wash it down. Unfortunately he was not a robust person and died at an early age.

WILLIE HENDERSON

Willie also lived in Claymires Lane, in the first house on the Brae. He was a tall, well built, cheery pleasant man, with some sort of disfigurement, resulting in one arm being shorter than the other.

However it seems this was no impediment as he was employed as a Booking Clerk at the Melrose Railway Station office of the London and North Eastern Railway Company. He was a keen follower of Melrose Rugby Football Club and held the post of Secretary for many years.

SARAH BROWN

Sarah was either a spinster or widow. Her abode was the tiny cottage by the roadside at the foot of Claymires Lane, now the property of Mrs Judy Schofield. The rear of the house at that time had a back door looking on to a track used by carts collecting the contents of the various middens, and Willie Slater's old ruined two storied dwelling house, long since gone.

Poor Sarah was either slightly mental or, perhaps senile, and was very much a recluse. At times the village boys when in the vicinity, for Willie Slater's house with its many swallows and other bird's nests to find, was a sort of adventure playground, unkindly teased her by knocking on her back door. Although this didn't happen often I always felt it to be harsh and uncaring.

MRS TULLOH

Mrs Tulloh was an English lady and the wife of Captain T A G Tulloh of Tannachie. The family came to the village shortly after the first world war. The previous occupants being the Lang family. Captain Lang was Adjutant of a Battalion of the Kings Own Scottish Borderers and went missing along with his Commanding Officer at Gallipoli. His name is on the village War Memorial.

The Tulloh's therefore occupied what was the principal house in Newstead, with extensive surrounding land and a cottage within its properties, known as Tannachie Cottage, and occupied by Mr Douglas the Coachman.

This was the only family of visible affluence, who could afford to employ domestic staff as well as a coachman and a pony and trap.

They considered themselves superior and attended the English

Church in Melrose, unlike the majority who were Church of Scotland inclined. Mrs Tulloh was a small woman, with obvious delusions of grandeur. She was always well dressed and accompanied by Pekinese dogs, but later acquired Dandy Dinmonts. She adopted a condescending deferential attitude when out walking, so was not given to mixing to any great degree with the natives. This drew from the older more perceptive villagers, some unkind criticism.

However, I remain extremely grateful for her kindness to me and prompt action which probably saved my eye sight from damage, after an accident. This arose when as a group of small boys, we had discovered a very active wasps nest on the Back Road. Our plan was to apply strong ammonia and destroy the wasps and nest. Ammonia was easy to come by, as all washing of clothes at home, was done in tubs with scrubbing boards, and it was used as a bleach. Willie Anderson produced a large jam jar of ammonia, and together we advanced to the nest, oblivious to the many numerous wasps on the wing.

Most country men are aware that the danger from bees and wasps is not from those which are returning homeward. The threat and danger comes from the insects emerging to do battle. So, as we approached with the ammonia, Willie was stung immediately, and several times, with the result that he threw the jar and ammonia by accident, into my eyes and face. I was in considerable pain, and completely blinded but somehow this quickly became apparent to Mrs Tulloh, as Tannachie was nearby. I was quickly taken in and dealt with by the lady herself, bathing my eyes and providing effective first aid.

This was a surprising and pleasing climax and revealed a hitherto unknown, but kindly disposition after all. So I cannot but look kindly on my memories of Mrs Tulloh.

DONALD McRITCHIE

Donald McRitchie was an old man, even when I knew him. He resided with his wife in the bottom half of a two storied house on the corner of Main Street, at its junction with the Yiddy Road.

The house has long since gone, and the area now contains a suggestion of a village green. Donald cultivated what is known as the Wellyard Garden, which lies at the bottom of the Wall Roadie right of way, and is now part of my property. The garden then contained, as it does today, a well, and there was another close by. The gate way was over grown and had an arch of ivy.

Although water had been introduced into Newstead in 1902, very few houses had indoor supplies, but seven public sources described as pumps, were situated at various points for easy access and the convenience of the villagers.

However, many of the houses had their individual wells or hand pumps, and in normal situations there was never a shortage of water. One could always borrow from a neighbour. It seems therefore that in 1920 there was a drought, and women were forced to draw water from wells normally not in use.

My recollection of this concerns Donald McRitchie, who was resisting common access to the well in his garden, and had locked the garden gate accordingly. Although very young I remember clearly irate housewives carrying white enamel buckets queuing up at the gate demanding access to the well. Donald was disputing this but was compelled to allow them in.

Seems such an insignificant event to remain in my memory for seventy seven years.

GEORDIE BALLANTYNE

Geordie lived in Addey Cottage on the Yiddy Road. He was a tall strong man, carrying on his trade as a joiner in East Port, Melrose. He was well liked and popular and something of a sportsman, having played rugby for Melrose in his young days.

His garden with its garden shed and numerous beehives was in the Yiddy Road opposite Addey Cottage. This is now completely gone, and has become a park for motor cars.

Geordie was a popular villager and compassionate enough to escort his Newstead friend the German hairdresser Herman Hansen to his shop in Abbey Street, Melrose, during the first world war. Hansen was disliked and frequently the subject of attacks and much abuse as local feelings ran high against German national. So Geordie Ballantyne is well remembered.

There are of course many ancients who have coloured village life over the years, all contributing to its character, but the few described may just provide a flavour of the times.

CONFLAGRATION AND COMPASSION

The Eildon hills are part of the Duke of Buccleuch's estates. In my early days, in order to preserve the grazing areas, and restrict the ever encroaching whin bushes, burning was an annual occurrence. This was applied equally to the Gattonside hills. The Buccleuch staff however controlled the burning, the timing of it designed for the protection of nesting wild life, and to control and limit its extent. In particular the direction of the wind was a major factor.

However, the Eildon hills operators, frequently encountered competition from village boys eager for the excitement induced by big fires, and a mild flouting of the law.

The trio of hills had been given distinctive names by the locals. The north, and the largest was known as the Newstead Hill. The shale covered central, of more volcanic appearance became the Melrose hill, and the southerly less steep heather covered feature was simply the Bowden Hill.

The hills in the early 1920's were the focus of much local activity. They were popular with walkers and climbers. Courting couples frequented the slopes, and hidden enclaves provided for many amorous encounters, so they became a Mecca for all sorts of young and old. Picnics were common.

The area also was grazed by sheep, and was cultivated in certain areas on the Newstead Hill, by Geordie Smith from Dingleton Mains farm. Although long since abandoned the field outlines are still visible today, from Newstead village. They were of course enclosed by red shale dry stone walls.

The views from the heights were exhilarating, and on a clear day it was possible to see Berwick and the sea. Unlike today, wild life abounded on the hills. The woods were populated by red squirrels, grey's were unknown. Skylarks rose and sang in the sky, Meadow Pipits, Whinchats, Stone Chats, Redstarts and Wheaters were in abundance. Linnets nested in the whins, Grouse grazed the heather, and blue, as well as multicoloured butterflies were commonplace. Predators seemed to be confined to Kestrels preying on voles and small birds, and weasels on the rabbits and hares. Cuckoos in the Spring were in competition with the many Corncrakes in the meadows. Blue berries attracted pickers and bee keepers brought their hives in the Autumn to reap the heather honey harvest. Raspberries in the fox covert were also a favourite attraction. The Buccleuch Hunt also attended the hill areas regularly.

This idyllic picture and the many happy hours spent there remains forever in my memory.

So, one sunny day, when the whins and surrounding dry grassland were in a suitable condition, and the wind in favourable direction, some of the local boys set fire to the whins. Unexpectedly the wind changed, and the initial small conflagration extended to other areas and the surrounding heather. The heavy smoke became visible for miles, and Geordie Smith the farmer, as well as the Melrose Fire Brigade were soon alerted.

Geordie Smith, with two collie dogs were observed approaching swiftly, so the boys searched in a panic for some sort of concealment. With Geordie's attention distracted by the fierce fire, and fearing recognition, they lay hidden amongst the smoke, with the dogs fortunately more interested in the sheep.

The Melrose Fire Brigade was a part time service, manned by local artisans, who as volunteers, on hearing the alarm left their places of employment. The firemen this day were, Jim Bunyan, Tommy Dodds, Charlie Mitchell and Bob Cowe amongst others. They eventually discovered the boys, who were of course well known, and realising the situation and the implications shepherded them quickly into the cab of the fire engine, and out of sight of the angry farmer.

When the fires had been extinguished and the fire engine was returning to the station, which was beside the local police station, the miscreants anxiety increased. the consequences of police interest, and the proximity of the police office to their likely point of debussment, raised much fear. However, it seemed the firemen had compassion, and a sympathetic view of boyish pranks, so a detour was made through Buccleuch Street, where they were deposited with an admonition, and advice not to disclose the outcome or, that they had been anywhere near the Hills.

Such understanding and benevolence was a common feature of country life in those times.

NICKNAMES OR NOMES DE PLUME

A distinctive feature of local life in my early days was a common use of nicknames. In Newstead I recall only a few, but Melrose provided an astonishing assembly of strange characters, and consequently in the prevailing atmosphere of the times, they attracted to themselves some old unusual titles.

The reasons for this probably derive from a combination of factors. Harsh living conditions, an absence of daily newspapers, no radio or television, and a desire to provide some aspect of self entertainment and humour. Eccentric behaviour, unfortunate incidents reflecting adversely and leading to embarrassment also contributed

Certainly the various names bestowed on the unfortunates were intended to identify them permanently. In Newstead the few I recall were 'Tag' Tulloh, 'Wicked' Willie Clark, 'Clippy' Scott, 'Mud' Miles, 'Titch' and his older brother 'Curn' Mitchell. 'Tag' derived from Captain Tulloh's initials, 'Wicked' Willie from an uncertain temper, and 'Clippy' from an unfortunate hair cut. 'Titch' was of course tiny and 'Curn' described the colour of Charlie Mitchell's hair.

Melrose however had a proliferation of personalities, where sources or reasons for nicknames defy reasonable logic. A random recollection comes to mind in 'Toosh' Cook, 'Toddy' Dodds, 'Hairy' McGregor, 'Powk' Lawrie, 'Binkie' Sinclair, 'Bung' Bunyan, 'Bowie' Allan, 'Tout' McLaren, 'Tidy' Mercer, 'Midge' Bassett and his mother 'Teeny'. Others were Jock the Gonger, Bob the Dobbler, 'Tory' Knox, 'Tob' Lillico and Jock O' the forge. 'Baggie' Slater, 'Stiltie' Lockie, 'Spankie' McDougall, 'Jockie' Blecknin, 'Eckie' Boo, 'Tilly' Rob and Pop Ticket. Jock 'Whitey' Whitworth are others that come to mind. 'Jock the Rip' Redpath, 'Snuffy' Jeemes, 'Tittle' Brown, 'Piper' McKenzie, 'Jimmy the Snob' and one strange one 'Santoy'. There were many others.

'Toosh' Cook lived in Dingleton. He was often seen in Melrose in his wheelchair, having been badly wounded in the first world war, the nickname is unusual. A common expression at that time was fantouche, thought to imply smart or posh. 'Toddy' Dodds was a plumber much given to a fondness for whisky toddy. 'Bowie' Allan was inclined to be bow legged.

'Tout' McLaren acquired his nickname when he was accosted in Abbey Street, returning from fishing in the Tweed. When asked how he had got on, he replied, "Only two tout and a baggie minnow".

'Hairy' McGregor was our school master. The 'Gonger' was Jock Crawford, a baker to trade. 'Binkie' Sinclair was one of a family of clothiers and gents outfitters in the Melrose Square. 'Tob' Lillico was a road sweeper but a native of Tobermory.

The 'Rip' was Jock Redpath, who had a wooden leg. He drove a coal lorry for Lawrie the coal merchant, and eventually married one of the Lawrie daughters. He was always boasting about the produce from his garden. "Tatties!, tatties!, tatties as big as your heid!" was his common cry. So when the Melrose Horticultural show was being held in the Corn Exchange, and Jock was seen approaching, one of the local wags called out "take the doors off the Corn Exchange, here's Jock Ripath coming with his cabbages!" Such was life in Melrose.

'Bob the Dobbler' was Bob McVittie, an unsavoury squint eyed character, who gained notoriety exposing himself to women.

'Teeny' Bassett was one day making her way down the High Street, when a passing coal lorry shed a large lump of coal. Living in a fair degree of poverty, she dashed across the road to retrieve it. However, Mr Scott the baker, with a shop near Burt's Hotel, had also observed the treasure, and before 'Teeny' could reach the scene, he had it safely rescued for himself.

In Melrose however, nicknames were not confined to individuals alone. St Dunstans was known as 'The Wilderness' and Abbey Street 'The Bow'.

Gattonside too was not devoid of characters. Tommy Boston had a famous talking dog, and old Jimmy Dodds claimed that 'honesty is the best policy' because "I've tried them baith and a' ken!". Those happy days of fun and frolics, alas, are gone forever.

PISCATORIAL PARADISE POSTPONED

Although originally a native of Newtown, Jock McKenzie was well known in Newstead. There are various reasons for this. After moving to live in the village early in life, he left for many years, returning to settle until his death. He also attracted a certain notoriety as the forgetful ambulance driver at Newstead Hospital whose inattention and lack of responsibility left Mrs McGinnis locked in the ambulance garage overnight. An action which somehow was forgiven by the authorities.

The villagers were not endeared to him, particularly because his unsociable attitude and behaviour, coupled with a readiness to inform to the police, became perceived as a misplaced loyalty to his fellow villagers.

The exaggerated tales of his exploits in the army in India, and outrageous and unbelievable catches of fish he had taken from the Tweed, all stamped Jock in the eyes of the villagers, as a charlatan and mountebank.

He was often exposed; once particularly by Dr Bill Blackstock of the Millhouse. He had been bragging to the Doctor of his Indian frontier exploits and disclosed that he had many photographs to prove it. When Dr Blackstock saw the photos of Jock in uniform, he remarked that Jock didn't appear to be wearing any medals. Finding himself caught out, Jock dismissed the criticism, claiming that medals were not issued to troops in his day.

On another occasion when a rotten Ash tree had fallen in a garden and an old man was cutting it up, Jock's attitude was typical when he was over heard saying "Report the bugger"!

He was a difficult resident in an ancient village with many related families, so any opportunity to deflate him was received with great glee.

One day, whilst playing in the Yiddy, some of the local urchins spotted Jock fishing for trout in the Tweed. He was wading with water just up to his ankles, whistling an old regimental tune and casting his line in anticipation.

Now, most country boys carried catapults, and were proficient and accurate in their use, so for fun and devilment, some small stones were gathered and Jock's fishing area became a target. The small whinstones were aimed first out of casting reach, and Jock, imagining that fish were feeding and that a rise was on, kept moving ever forward.

The river bed is not however a level surface, and Jock's gradual advance and loss of concentration was swiftly interrupted when upon stepping into a deep hole, he lost his balance and his rod, which quickly floated down stream towards Leaderfoot.

The boys by this time, much amused, withdrew homewards, and the tale was told in one particular household, of the boy who fired the catapult. An older member of this large family later was drinking in the Ship Inn at Melrose, when Jock McKenzie entered for his evening glass of whisky. In the general conversation Jock, in his usual fashion, elaborated on how, when fishing earlier at Newstead, there had been a fantastic rising of fish, and how he had caught twenty huge trout in as many minutes. this created great interest in the bar, but many enquiries about the name of the fly he was using didn't deflect Jock's exaggerations, until a voice in the background was heard to mutter, "It's just another bloody great lie!".

Jock McKenzie is now with his 'maker', and the memories will fade with time, but, like so much of the old village life will soon be just a thing of the past.

THE FALSE ALARM

Gattonside House was occupied pre war by the Montgomery family. They were wealthy aristocrats, employing a large staff, and related to the Earl of Eglinton in Ayrshire. They kept horses and hunted regularly. The head groom was Peter Cosgrove, an Englishman and small of stature. He had an assistant who also came from south of the Border.

At weekends, Gattonside society not provided with a public house in the village, was consequently attracted to the various Melrose hostelries. Peter Cosgrove and his henchman regularly, especially at weekends made the short journey from Gattonside village to Melrose, via the suspension bridge over the river Tweed, known locally as the Chain Bridge, or 'Cheen Brig'.

On one particular Saturday night following a round of the Melrose public houses, where 'nips' and 'pints' were the common form of liquid alcohol consumption in those days, they made their way back to Gattonside in a slightly distressed condition. On crossing the chain bridge with its undulating movement, Peter became very sick, and consequently the river Tweed flowing below became a convenient repository.

Having finally reached home in Gattonside safely, he awoke on the Sunday morning, unable to find his false teeth. After some deliberation and retracing the previous night's movements, it was assumed that the missing teeth may now be lying in the river under the bridge. Accompanied by his assistant he returned to the scene, and indeed it was discovered that something seen gleaming in some weeds in the river below could possibly be the missing teeth.

Peter then, guided by directions from his friend on the bridge above, waded into the river and retrieved with great joy a set of false teeth. Giving them a slosh or two in the water to clean them, he put them back into his mouth, only to find they didn't fit. Cursing he called out to his companion, "The bloody teeth are not mine"!, and in a rage hurled them over the river bank.

Now very despondent, Peter felt that the only course now open was a visit to McLaren the dentist, and a new set of dentures, although the resulting expense was very much on his mind.

A few days later when accosted coming down the 'Bow', the local name for Abbey Street, by a friend who had learnt of his misfortune, Peter was found to be in possession of a smart set of teeth. When the friend remarked that McLaren the dentist had moved pretty fast in producing new teeth, Peter then, with a smile revealed that he had not after all lost his teeth over the 'cheen brig', but that his daughter had found them under his bed at home in Gattonside.

JOE SNOWIE

For whatever the reason, be they harsh working conditions, low wages, poor home and environmental facilities or inadequate education, the populace in Newstead and Melrose threw up many quaint individuals.

There was a distinct lack of entertainment, as is available today. Eccentric behaviour, foolish remarks, allied to the common use of nicknames, all contributed to produce much amusement, and further emphasis on the notoriety of particular characters.

The term 'worthies' became common place.

One such then, was Joe Snowie, who I have referred to in another article, assuring some American visitors that there were no lions or tigers on the Eildon hills. Joe ran a coal merchants business from the back station at Melrose, where the coal wagons were shunted into a siding. He also accepted various contracting arrangements with his horses. Jock Hamilton frequently used his services as a cabby, driving American visitors from the Hamilton hotels, around the Scott country. Strong drink added to Joe Snowie's problems, and his wife resented this. There were frequent squabbles and much unhappiness. The Snowie's occupied a house at Danielton Cottages in Dingleton.

On one particularly wet and windy night, Joe arrived home late in his usual inebriated state, on hearing his approach Mrs Snowie promptly locked the door, and refused his entrance. After some considerable shouting through the door from both sides, including some strong language, Joe eventually withdrew.

After a suitable lapse of time, and some contemplation he decided on a cunning plan of action. Returning, he tapped gently on the door, and Mrs Snowie from the inside, asked "who's there?". Joe, adopting the voice of his church minister answered, "This is Mr – – – – –" giving the minister's name. "Do you know that your dearly beloved and loving husband Joseph Snowie is standin' oot here drookit in the bloody rain?"

When the Highland show visited Newstead, Joe was given the

contract to transfer goods and stores to the Annay Road site from the railway station, in his horse and cart. His attention to business was intermittent, and he was often found before midday, lying in the field flat out with his cap over his face. The Highland Show, which was a great success seemed however to have overcome any supply difficulties from this behaviour.

Another of Joe's contracts involved dragging trees out of a forest near Stow. Finding himself short of money for his drinking affliction, Joe sent a request to his wife in Dingleton. The story was that the white horse had died, and to fulfil the contract he would have to buy a replacement horse. Cash was duly sent.

Many months later when visiting St Boswells Fair, with Joe, Mrs Snowie immediately recognised the old white horse. It was now in the possession of gypsies who were attempting to sell it at the horse market.

There are of course many more stories of Joe's exploits, but those few will provide a flavour of the times. They all contributed to local, self made amusements, not readily forgotten, but unfortunately fading with age.

AULD CLEGGIE

John Cleghorn was a bachelor. He lived in a tenement at the East Port in Melrose, on the south side of the road, opposite Brown the joiner. The site of the house now demolished is presently occupied by a small car park. His neighbours at that time were the Crawfords, and the Pringles, the latter family subsequently moving to Hawthorn Cottage in the back road at Newstead. He was known simply as 'Cleggie', and was employed as a carter.

His quarters were a mere 'Butt and Ben', untidy, spartan and almost devoid of normal household chattels. There were no pictures to decorate the walls, and only a solitary chair to sit on. By the fireplace on the fender rested a brown teapot, with a broken spout. The mantel-piece was equally bare, graced only by a mug without a handle and an empty McEwan beer bottle, holding a half burnt candle. His bed was of the old fashioned 'cotter' type, set back in a special recess in the wall. The bed coverings consisted of numerous old army greatcoats. The house was also infested with mice and rats which had chewed holes in the only wardrobe. On the table lay an old cook book by Mrs Beaton.

Despite the obvious drawbacks, Cleggie was apparently inclined to vanity, because before appearing in public, he was wont to rouge his cheeks. Some people thought this was the application of beetroot juice, but I recall also seeing a suggestion of cream face powder. Needless to say, this attracted much attention and derision from the locals. Cleggie, like many of his kind, was fond of a drink and frequented the nearby Ship Inn. His principal boozing companions were Jock Pringle and 'Wull' Rutherford, and their regular carousing, sometimes rowdy, became a feature of East Port Life. After one particular night of over indulgence, Cleggie slipped off home, leaving his companions to continue drinking.

Jock Pringle was a notorious poacher, disposing of his salmon and other game in the Ship Inn, and frequently carried around his shotgun. Eventually when time was called, and they were about to leave, 'Wull' Rutherford reminded Jock that he had promised to sweep Cleggie's lum (chimney).

At this, Jock realised his commitment and departed, promising it would only take a few minutes. He approached Cleggie's house, still carrying his gun, and on pushing open the door, found old Cleggie fast asleep. Pointing the gun up the chimney he then fired both barrels. This immediately had a devastating effect bringing down much soot and masonry, enveloping both room and poor Cleggie in his bed.

The explosion and subsequent noise alerted Bob Brown, the joiner, who quickly arrived at the scene. Jock Pringle, by this time departed hurriedly to his home in Newstead. Cleggie, being completely stunned, shocked, and covered in soot, surveyed the scene and asked "what the hell has happened Bob, has the bloody war really started?". Bob Brown, unaware of the true cause, suggested that maybe the chimney had fallen down, and that it really was requiring attention from Jim Crawford the builder. Old Cleggie however, was still sceptical and unamused by remarks about his appearance, and the mess. Much laughter and references to 'Sambo', 'Al Jolson' and the 'Black and White Minstrels' did nothing to mollify the situation.

However, when the true story unfolded, Jock Pringle's involvement came as no surprise. There is a moral to this story. If you want to have your chimney swept, it's safer to do it yourself!

AVIAN IMPOSTOR

In 'Fur and Feather', I have described how many of the Newstead boys had tame Jackdaws as pets. It was a common sight to see those birds perched on the handlebars of a travelling bicycle, or flying nosily behind to catch up on the moving owner.

Jock Pringle, although not a boy, had in addition to a dog and many ferrets, a captive crow. Jock was often in need of money to satisfy his likeness for whisky, a similar problem affected his great chum and companion, 'Wull' Rutherford.

Together they frequented the numerous pubs in Melrose, but notably the Abbey Hotel and the Ship Inn. In the latter it seems it was easier to dispose of salmon, pheasants etc., acquired during their many poaching activities. Jock, being a mason to trade had access to bricks and they also could be sold for cash.

Jock Hamilton owned the Abbey Hotel, and was a genial landlord. He was an enormous man, well over 20 stones in weight, and this severely restricted his mobility, to the extent that he had difficulty in walking. He would sit behind the bar, dispensing to customers, and consuming himself large quantities of beer and whisky. He was particularly interested in coloured foreign birds. On the stairway of the hotel, a large glass case of stuffed birds occupied a prominent situation, augmented by a live African grey parrot, in a cage at one end of the bar.

Jock Pringle and 'Wull' Rutherford, hoping to raise some cash, and partly one suspects as a prank, thought up the idea of painting the pet crow. This was of course the easiest part of the project. Convincing Jock Hamilton to buy it was not going to be so easy. They painted the crow's back yellow, and the tail bright red, the head was coloured green and its breast crimson.

At the hotel entrance 'Wull' Rutherford observed through the window, that Jock Hamilton was in a suitable state of inebriation, and gave the signal for Jock Pringle to enter with the bird. The hotel lighting at that time was by gas, and not particularly bright. He strolled casually into the bar, and said to Jock Hamilton "I have something for you", and pulling the cover from the cage, revealed the colourful crow.

Aware of the two individuals, and their enjoyment of pranks, it is unlikely that Jock Hamilton was fooled, and going along with the situation, he quickly replied that it would make a nice present for his wife, and asked how much he wanted for it. The answer was "oh, next to nothing, a fiver will do". On pocketing the money, Jock Pringle withdrew and joined by 'Wull' Rutherford proceeded to the Ship Inn, where the tale was told amidst much amusement. The money was spent on drink.

The following day however, in daylight, and in the heat of the sun, the paint on the bird started to run. By now Jock Hamilton was not amused, and was heard to say "I'll get that pair of buggers yet!" but, having gone along with the prank, he expected that at least they should have spent the money at the Abbey Hotel, and not at his rivals at the ship Inn.

This true story is yet another example of how truth can be stranger than fiction!

APPOSITE OR APOCRYPHAL

In this area at least, eighty years ago, it was common for children to leave school at 14 years of age. So, for many the education thus attained often left something to be desired, whilst others made their way about the world with great success.

For those less than blessed with average intelligence, lifes burden and experiences, frequently involved them in accidents, where ignorance or naiveté led to comic situations.

These were seized upon by the locals and developed into elaborated tales, mostly to the detriment of the individual concerned. They remain as shadows attached, but strangely, not of a condemnatory nature. They were intended to provide amusement.

One particular native son of Melrose attracted such attention, following gaffes relating to motor cars. In the early days of the motor car, mechanical knowledge, especially to the layman owner, was scanty indeed. Only trained garage workmen appeared as experts.

Thus, the individual concerned with his newly acquired vehicle arrived at a local garage complaining that he was having trouble. The mechanic upon lifting the bonnet made a quick inspection of the plugs, and remarked "Oh I think there is a plug missing". The response came quickly, "Now, who the hell could have taken that?" This show of ignorance soon became common knowledge in the community, and the source of much amusement.

Another story was soon to be added. This involved the car being repaired, when the garage owner informed him it required a new halfshaft, "oh, just put on a whole one" was the answer.

Yet another time he stopped his car in order to give a lift to a passenger going into town. The excessive speed of travel alarmed the passenger who enquired why he was driving so fast, the answer given was that the car was short of petrol, and he wanted to reach a garage before it ran out.

This well known individual who could barely write his name, subsequently became a very successful business man in Melrose. Although he died young, and many years ago, the stories still prevail.

SELF SUFFICIENCY

Between the wars, unemployment was high and wages a meagre few pounds a week. Apprentices often were paid just seven shillings and six pence. The "old age pension" nowadays termed retirement pension, had not been introduced, so the Newstead villagers had, of necessity to look towards some sort of self support.

Every garden, whatever its size was cultivated and vegetables grown and fruit trees of all sorts harvested. I have described how Bella Scott, from the shop had the "Cockit Hat" garden at the junction of the Leaderfoot and Broomhill roads. Davie Forrest the signalman at Ravenswood railway junction, where the main line to Earlston joined the main line, kept a large garden there, which he cultivated in his spare time, between the passing of the trains.

This photograph shows an onion harvest at Fortune Row.

NEWSTEAD ANCIENTS REMEMBERED

John Bell (Miller) and family	Newstead Mill
Mr Purves and family	Millmount Farm
Sandy Ross (Ploughman)	Thatched Cottage, by Tweedside
Duncan McKinnon and family	Mill Cottages
Herman Hanson and family	Mill Cottages
John Cowie and family	Mill Cottages
Mrs Geddes and Norman (Fur Farm)	Newstead Mill
Mr Moffat and Housekeeper	Saugh Cottage
Johnny Douglas and family	Tannachie Cottage
The Alchin family and Willie	Old Floishers Shop
The Biggar family and Tom	Main Street
The Linton family and Agnes	Main Street
The Ormiston family	Main Street
Bill Tait and the Girls	Rikki Burn
Mr Henderson (an Albino)	West End Cottage
The Thompson family with Peggy, Rena and Ina	West End Cottage
Johnny Cathray	Beatties Corner
	(House demolished)
Donald McRitchie	Beatties Cottage
	(House demolished)
Jock Davidson, wife and Mary	Rothesay Cottage
Geordie Ballantyne and Ivy	Addey Cottage
Jock Ford, wife with Nell and Jenny	Yiddy Road
Jenny Miller, Spinster and deaf	Hawthorn Cottage
Tommy Wight, wife with Iris and Tom	Main Street
Dave Forrest, wife with John, Jim and Alex	Eildon View
Ralph Davidson, wife with Sheila	Main Street

Fred Hart and sister	Burnside Cottage
Willie Mitchell, wife with Sonny and Annie	Burnfoot
Miss Sewell and Miss McCartney (Deaconesses)	Deaconess House
Mrs Cleaver, Beatrice, John and Willie	Fairfax Cottage
Peter Nisbet, wife with Meg	The Auld Hoose
Bella McKenzie (shopkeeper)	Burnfoot
Bill Scott and family with Annie	Briar Cottage
Wat Borthwick and family with Jim, Sid, Wat and Janet	St John's Cottage
Tom Mitchell and family	St John's Cottage
Jim Gill and family with Ella and Jennie	Dove Cottage
Jock Chapman and family with Bill and Jennie	Cairnhill
Jim Hardie with Mother	Thatched House, East End
The Riddell family with May	Townhead Farm
Jim Ford and family	Barnethead Farm
Bob Turnbull	Railway Cottage
Bob Anderson and family of fifteen	Roselea
Old Jim Pringle	Hawthorn Cottage
Jock Pringle, wife with Helen, Maud and Gladys	Hawthorn Cottage
Captain Tulloh and family	Tannachie
Miss Vietch and sister	Hazledean
Grannie Ovens and Sid	Claymires Cottage
Mrs McGuiness, Sandy and Bill	Claymires Cottage

and many others

CONCLUSION

So Goethe took sixty years to write '*Faustus*'!

The foregoing few notes about old Newstead have taken me some sixty days. The equivalent in mental expression however is probably comparable. I have found it, to be at times both stimulating and exciting, and confining nostalgia to the mind and memory ensures and manifests pleasurable reminiscence. On the other hand a physical return to recall old joys and scenes leads to much disillusionment, despair and disappointment. The motto therefore should be "never go back". Better to retain the fond memories as they remain, forever etched in the mind. There is so much more to be told of Old Newstead, but if the few notes herewith, convey just a flavour of the past life and characters, and are appreciated by interested readers, then I will take some small satisfaction from it all.

In the words of Edith Piaf's song "No, no, regrets"!

Jim Gordon
1996